Decorating with Flowers

Text by DENISE OTIS
Flower Design by RONALDO MAIA
Photographs by ERNST BEADLE

Decorating with Flowers

Harry N. Abrams, Inc., Publishers, New York

Editor: Margaret L. Kaplan

Designer: Wei-Wen Chang

Library of Congress Cataloging in Publication Data

Otis, Denise.
   Decorating with flowers.
   1. Flower arrangement. I. Maia, Ronaldo, joint
author. II. Beadle, Ernst, joint author. III. Title.
SB449.M328   745.92   78-5243
ISBN 0-8109-0808-5

Library of Congress Catalogue Card Number: 78-5243

Published in 1978 by Harry N. Abrams, Incorporated, New York
All rights reserved. No part of the contents of this book may be
reproduced without the written permission of the publishers

Printed and bound in Japan

Contents

NOTE by Ronaldo Maia

A flower for me is special and I always try to find a special space for it. I don't use flowers to decorate, I use them for happiness. To bring life, form, and beauty into the midst of the things we love. Working with flowers for me is a way to show my love for the world. It is the force of inspiration for everything I do.

I don't arrange flowers, I try to interpret nature. The elements that I use are forms from nature: the luxuriance that explodes and fills the eye, the simplicity of one line inside a space. Nature teaches us that everything has a cycle—flowers germinate, grow, blossom, drop their petals and leaves—and that nothing is wasted. Leaves and petals in the forest create humus, in the house, potpourri.

I wish to dedicate my contribution to this volume to life, the only way to learn beauty. To God, the provider of the creation around us. To balance and the harmony that leads to simplicity. To all that I love.

And I wish to dedicate it to Senhor Geraldo A. Maia and Dona Isotta Pezzi Maia, my parents, from whom I got my values. To my very special friends. To Frederick Crowell and Rose Cumming for opening a door. To Setsuo Kitano. To my clients, who encourage me. To Ernst Beadle with his third eye, and to Denise Otis, who does with words what I try to do with flowers.

Introduction

Flowers have such a spontaneous appeal that it is sometimes hard to remember that nature produces them for a practical purpose and not just to give us pleasure. Pleasure we need never be without, since every season of the year brings them in a seemingly endless variety of colors and forms and fragrances. We can even have the seasons we want when we want them, thanks to modern flower technology and air transport. Few if any of the ornaments that we can use to enhance our surroundings are so accessible to everyone, so enjoyable to work with, and so easy to integrate into any kind of room or style of decoration. Decorating with flowers is an art with very simple requirements: a love of flowers and the willingness to experiment.

This may seem an unusual attitude for a professional designer in flowers and particularly for one of the stars of the profession. But Ronaldo Maia is known for the unexpected. Whether they are spectacular and individual fantasies or simple and natural enough to seem artless, his designs start trends. They are regularly reported in newspapers and magazines. Ronaldo, who was born and brought up in Brazil, works in a way that is fresh, original, and appropriate to the way we live today. Clients from Europe and all over North and South America, including several museums and many of New York's best-known hostesses, seek out his shop in New York. Although he can draw on a wide range of training and extensive study of seventeenth- and eighteenth-century European flower arrangement and garden design, he firmly believes that "it is only by living and working with flowers that you train your eye and liberate your imagination." His designs are all informed with a deep love and understanding of growing things, and many of his arrangements have an almost childlike simplicity—a quality that he feels flowers have. Even the fantasies he creates depend more on fresh intuitions and inventive combinations of plant materials than they do on elaborate techniques. The *New York Times* called his work the most unusual of all the super flower designers.

Flowers, for Ronaldo, are finished nature-made ornaments that really want only the simplest, most natural of presentations and the simplest, least obtrusive of containers to work their magic in a room. The whole subject of placing flowers in containers seems to have acquired an aura of needless complexity, which may be a matter of the words we use—an accepted and inescapable vocabulary. We talk about making arrangements or compositions and this can seem a rather daunting undertaking if your instant mental image of a flower arrangement is of something very complicated or stylized. In fact, when you cut even one flower and place it in a container you have created an arrangement, a composition, of flower and container. And if it pleases your eye, a successful one. If not, then you adjust it until it does. Is the flower too tall for the container? Cutting the stem is the answer. Or too short, too large, or too small? Are the colors not harmonious? In all these cases a different container will solve the problem. With more flowers the eye has more judgments to make, but the arranging process remains simple and straightforward.

When you begin thinking of flowers as objects of art in themselves, arranging any kind, whether you have one or an armload—a single rose or fifty—is just a matter of finding a container that will show to best advantage its particular shape and color and texture. Placing your arrangement in a room, like placing any decorative object, is a question of experimenting until you find the location where it contributes most attractively to the whole environment. This takes attention to the relationship of flower, container, and setting, but it is the easiest approach to arranging and decorating with flowers, and the least time-consuming. It is one Ronaldo is fond of, and it can be so effective that you may never wish to take any other.

All those beautiful shapes and colors and textures are very tempting to the imagination, however, and the impulse to combine and shape them into ornaments of your own design is almost irresistible. Although they are living things and take gentle handling, flowers are among the most accommodating—and least expensive—of raw materials for the exercise of your creative instincts. We often fall into the habit of thinking of them as luxuries, perhaps because they are short-lived. We should not. Flowers do not have to be rare or out-of-season, hence costly, to be worth our attention. Some of the humblest weeds have extraordinarily attractive forms and colors. Indeed, almost every plant in nature has some ornamental potential. And in a decorative medium, evanescence has its advantages: it encourages a light-hearted playing with ideas that stimulates creativity; gives generous opportunities for practice, which brings confidence and skill; and bestows on your surroundings the zest and refreshment of variety.

As a source of ideas for designing with flowers, nature is inexhaustible, and for additional inspiration paintings and sculpture, prints and photographs offer the flower decorations of every period and culture. Particular traditions and styles of flower arranging have their own conventions—Japanese tradition, English style, for example—and if one of them appeals to you, you may find learning about its conventions helpful. But whatever the source of the inspiration, it is more important that a design please you and create the effect you want than that it follow conventions. In decorating with flowers as in decorating with all the other elements that make up the furnishings of a house, the style of today is individualism.

Our rooms are personal museums of all the things that attract us or express our interests. If we are fond of a past style we adapt it to suit our own way of living. We choose objects and ideas from every time and place including our own and combine them in individual ways. When we call in a professional—an architect or decorator—we choose one whose style most closely resembles our own point of view.

Decorating with flowers is just as much a matter of personal expression and taste, and there is no one correct way to go about it. "You can't make rules for individuality," as Ronaldo points out. In any case rules, which are always proposed to be helpful, end up being inhibiting. What we have to offer in the following pages are ideas, and the designs of a talented and imaginative professional. Designs in a variety of moods—romantic, witty, architectural, and playful—for rooms of many different kinds and styles. Arrangements for everyday enjoyment, fantasies to create a feeling of festivity, and decorations for holidays, big parties, and celebrations. We tell you how and why the arrangements were made, explain the tools and techniques used, and share with you the tips and tricks that all of us—Ronaldo, photographer Ernst Beadle, and I—have learned in years of growing, arranging, and living with flowers. We hope that our ideas and experience will inspire and help you in your own exploration of the pleasures of living with flowers.

For their very real and much appreciated contribution to the existence of this book, we would like to thank Mr. and Mrs. Harcourt Amory, Jr., Kenneth Bates, Peter E. Bullough, Alan C. Greenberg, Dona Guimaraes, Eric Hurner, Richard H. MacKay, Mr. and Mrs. Alfred J. Moran, Jr., Mr. and Mrs. Walter Nelson Pharr, Mr. and Mrs. Andrew Stewart, Mr. and Mrs. Michael Hall Thomas, and Frederick Wehmer, all of whom generously allowed us to photograph in their houses or apartments; Mr. and Mrs. James DeWoody and Mr. and Mrs. Milton Silverman, who let us photograph the decorations for their weddings; and The Rouse Company, which let us photograph decorations for two of its parties. We would like to thank Mr. and Mrs. J. Hawley Otis for sharing with us their knowledge of growing and caring for flowers, and the many friends who contributed information and suggestions—in particular Carlotta E. Wick, who also typed the manuscript. We would also like to express our gratitude to Margaret L. Kaplan, our editor, and to Nai Y. and Wei-Wen Chang, the designers of this book, for their help, encouragement, and patience.

1. Concerning Containers

The container cabinet of a flower arranger with eclectic taste in containers. An antique Chinese basket shares the top of the cabinet with a blue-and-gray stoneware basin, a Japanese bronze flask, an Italian green glass compote, and two modern reproductions in white pottery of period flower containers—a Victorian tiered épergne and a seventeenth-century tulipière. On the top shelf: a gaily decorated heart-shaped spout vase based on an eighteenth-century design, a porcelain pitcher, and a variety of glass and ceramic vases. The shelf below holds a gourd with a bamboo base, a basket tray, two tin molds, a flared pewter tumbler, three containers in the Art Nouveau style—a gourd-shaped green glass vase, a leaf-patterned black one, a dark-green one swirled with tulips—and behind them, two simple glass cylinders, cobalt blue and clear. Assembled on the bottom shelf: a white flowerpot vase, classic Chinese designs in bronze and in white porcelain, a flat white stoneware bowl, a tall gray Swedish cut-crystal vase, a fat brass bowl, a green glass bud vase, a basket, and a modern terra-cotta container shaped like a burlap bag. On the floor are big baskets and stoneware crocks.

What the flowers are arranged in is just as much a part of an arrangement as the flowers. This is evident when the container is very decorative or very colorful, but even self-effacing vases, like the clear glass ones Ronaldo often uses for single flowers, influence the total effect. Their delicacy gives the flowers center stage, their transparency reveals the lines of the stems.

"There has to be a marriage between flowers and container. The whole design is these flowers in this container; change either and you have a different design. You have to live with flowers to learn what they will do, and you have to live with the things you put them in to find out how they work best for the flowers and for your house."

How do you go about choosing containers? There are so many considerations, practical and personal, that it is hard to give any answer without instantly wishing to qualify it. Even the necessity for a container is open to qualification. It seems obvious that once you cut a flower from its roots, it needs water for nourishment and something to support it—hence a container. But some flowers last a considerable time without water; very short-stemmed flowers may need no support; whether or not they are put in a container is purely a design decision. Camellias and gardenias—usually cut with the barest minimum of stem to spare the plant—last quite as well laid right on a table in flat garlands as they do composed in a low crystal bowl. Dried flowers do not want water and, tied in a sheaf like wheat, will support themselves. While containers are far more often needed than not, these examples—you can probably think of a dozen others—suggest how riddled with exceptions the whole subject of containers is. No discussion of them can be completely objective. Personal preferences are sure to creep in and they should. You decorate with flowers to give pleasure, and the materials you work with should give you pleasure as well. A collection of containers that one person finds continual enjoyment in using might offer no inspiration at all to another. There are so many things in which flowers can be successfully arranged, whether designed for that purpose or not, that we cannot hope to illustrate or mention all of them. What we will do is suggest certain kinds that we find particularly satisfying and offer some

◄◄ Wine and liquor bottles are an excellent source of recyclable containers. Miniatures are just right for single blossoms. Putting together a matched set would be a snap for anyone who travels often on planes.

◄ A miscellany of found containers. The tallest, which is particularly attractive for arrangements that include bending, trailing flowers like morning glories or clematis, once held preserved plums; the white glass one held Dijon mustard. In the foreground is a glass inkwell. The rest are old medicine and pill bottles picked out in antique and junk shops.

◄◄ Perfume bottles, so many of which are carefully designed and made, are among the most recyclable of all the containers that come into your house. When you find a clean, attractive shape with removable labeling and an opening large enough for the stem, you have a vase for a single flower.

◄ Clear glass vases for single flowers. Two are pharmaceutical glass, the Erlenmeyer flask clearly identified as such by its capacity markings. The unmarked boiling flask is almost impossible to distinguish from Ronaldo's bud vases, five of which he has epoxied together in a modern counterpart to the spout vases of ancient China and Persia. Simple shapes like these, whatever their provenance, are among the most versatile of flower containers.

general observations that we hope will help you to find those that are right for you.

Perhaps the most important thing to keep in mind is that cost has very little to do with how well a container plays its role in an arrangement. What counts are shape, size, color, and texture. To get the container you want for a certain flower or a certain kind of presentation you can spend almost any amount of money or nothing at all. Take for example a small vase for a single flower. A hand-blown bud vase of the finest crystal can be extremely beautiful. It can also be very expensive, particularly if you want more than one. The delicate clear glass vases Ronaldo uses cost considerably less. Less delicate and less expensive but still beautifully shaped are laboratory glass flasks and bottles—the best ones for flowers are those without graduated capacity markings. You can find other treasures at yard sales and in antique shops of the modest kind: blown-glass medicine bottles and vials that have lost their ground-glass stoppers, for example, often cost under a dollar. Or you can recycle and spend nothing. Look with an unprejudiced eye at every container that comes into your house and you will be surprised at how many good-looking possibilities there are. Among them are perfume bottles—if your preferences are consistent, assembling a matched set takes only time—and liquor miniatures, some of which have good, simple shapes and a rustic sort of charm.

Finding containers is a creative pursuit in itself, a constant challenge to the eye and the imagination. Given the budget, you can assemble a collection in which every piece is in itself a work of art in crystal or silver, pottery or porcelain, wood or stone, bronze or basketry. But there is great satisfaction in discovering beauty and congeniality in the simplest and least expensive of objects. There are so many places to look—craft exhibitions, gift and department stores, junk shops, flea markets and fairs where you would expect to find them, and a good many places where you would not. Kitchen, restaurant, and hospital suppliers reward exploration. And everyday grocery shopping can turn up prizes—wooden fruit and berry baskets,

◄ Recycled containers at work. Selected for their forms and not their contents, little bottles made for an ounce or two of spirits instead hold a daffodil apiece.

In place of a single large arrangement, a quartet of small ones decorates a Victorian shaving stand. One glass flask holds a tight nosegay of Queen Anne's lace in galax leaves perked up with a single blue pansy and a rakish plume of blue veronica. In its twin another blue veronica and two curving sprays of pink everlasting pea are also collared in galax. Bright pink verbenas in a white china vase and white petunias in a tumbler complete the array. In a free-and-easy composition like this, it matters little whether containers are mixed or matched in shape or material as long as they suit the sizes and colors of the flowers.

◄ The little spout vase fabricated from five glass bud vases holds a nosegay of freesia, alstroemeria, anemone, and Queen Anne's lace with a few lily of the valley leaves. An effortless arrangement for the container shapes the bouquet. Whether it is an open or compact one depends on the quantity of flowers used. Chinese porcelain parrots and a Chinese scroll painting make an appropriate setting—the oldest containers designed on this principle that we know are Chinese—but the allusion was unintentional and the vase has a simplicity that adapts it to any environment.

15

cheese crocks and boxes, stoneware or pottery mustard and jam pots are just a few examples.

Flower containers need not hold water as long as they can be lined with something that does. If you use florist's water-absorbent foam to hold the flowers, the liner may be no more than a piece of heavy plastic. When you use a basket or wooden container often, or when it is an old and valuable one, you will find it more convenient to have a permanent liner. For unusual or complicated shapes you may have to have one made by a local tinsmith, but usually it is not difficult to find a good fit ready-made. Plastic refrigerator containers and glass baking dishes, which come in a variety of round and rectangular shapes and sizes, are invaluable. One of the hazards of container collecting is that once in a while even those that are supposed to hold water fail to do their job. Always test a new container before you use it, and use a liner if there is any doubt.

With all the possibilities that present themselves, the big question is how to narrow the choices to manageable proportions. There are several points of view from which you can work. We will talk about each separately, but in fact none necessarily excludes another.

You can choose the places in your rooms where you would like to have flowers, then choose the containers for those places, and then choose flowers that are right for those containers. This was often done in history. In many great eighteenth-century rooms the vases were designed as part of the decoration and were never changed. The flowers changed with the seasons, but the relation between furniture, vase, and flowers was stable.

Shape and size are the first considerations in selecting containers for particular locations. One mantelpiece may look better with a long, low, narrow container in the center, another with a matched pair of urns at either end, a third with just one medium-size bowl placed to balance a painting or an arrangement of objects. One space in a room may call for a very tall vase, another for something low and rather massive. Sometimes it is easy to visualize exactly what you need, sometimes you have to find it by experimenting. In experimenting, improvised containers are a great help, and a fine source for them is the kitchen. A big brown mixing bowl may be a bit too rustic as a permanent inhabitant of the hall table, but trying it there once, filled with masses of chrysanthemums, can tell you if it has the shape and size you would enjoy in that spot. Or a breadbasket packed with little ferns may help you reach a decision about outfitting the mantelpiece.

The style or period in which your house is decorated will influence your choice of containers—certain vase forms seem characteristically Victorian or Empire or modern—but need not determine it. Simple classic shapes have a way of making themselves at home in almost any room, whatever the spirit of its furnishings. And at times contrast is more exciting than carefully planned authenticity. A particular dining room comes to mind, sparely, sleekly modern—white walls, white marble tables, steel-and-leather chairs, brilliant abstract paintings—where the flower container, to magnificent effect, was a wildly ornate rococo silver tureen.

Compatibility of color and texture is more important than period. And for all the exuberance of its ornament, the tureen shared both sheen and precision of workmanship with its soberly designed companions. Rough earthenware, coarse baskets, crudely carved stone usually seem uncomfortable in a room furnished in delicate colors and textures, and so do fine porcelains in a rustic cottage or in the kitchen. Usually, but not always. Like all general guidelines, this one is open to exceptions and special cases.

Color is an even more complex subject. The less colorful the container, the wider the range of flower colors that will look well in it. The natural tones of wood, straw, stone, and metal; neutral blacks, whites, grays; pale soft greens like celadon give the greatest flexibility in choosing flowers. But then a container whose color echoes one in a painting or a fabric, or accents by contrast, often contributes greatly to the decoration of a room. It simply limits the flower colors you can use in it; the more intense the color of the container, the more limiting it is. Still more difficult to fit flowers to are highly patterned or ornamented vases, particularly multicolored ones.

Mauve stock and pink peonies in an off-white stoneware crock. The bouquet is a simple one, depending for its interest on the colors and the contrasting forms of the flowers.

◄ White rhododendron in a soft-pink cube. Only enough leaves are left on each short branch to give a sense of the separate flower clusters; the rest have been removed for both looks and longevity—the only technique involved in an otherwise simple, natural arrangement. Two Indonesian palm-leaf fans, leaves of another kind, are balanced behind the vase to give the flowers a frame.

They can be extremely beautiful, and when they are they usually work better as art objects than as flower containers. However, if flexibility is less important to you than your pleasure in the container, you can look at the limitations imposed by color or pattern as challenges and find ways to meet them. Two very successful solutions come instantly to mind: one, a brilliant yellow vase that harbors a succession of white flowers, sometimes by themselves, sometimes with the addition of a few blossoms—daffodils, freesia, daylilies—in the same glowing shade of yellow. The other, a monumental many-colored Chinese jar that always holds a carefully composed arrangement of branches, berried or bare ones in autumn and winter, sparsely flowered quince or dogwood in spring, beech or maple in summer.

If adjusting your choice of flowers to specific containers in specific places seems too restrictive, you can build your collection the other way round and let the flowers come first. Selecting containers to suit favorite flowers and combinations, then finding or making a place to put the bouquets is another approach to consider. Few rooms today are so stylized or rigidly arranged that placement is a problem. In fact, the minor regroupings involved are a pleasant and easy way to refresh your surroundings.

"To find the right containers for the flowers you like," Ronaldo stresses, "it helps to see how they grow. From their growth you get an idea of the kind of container that will have the right balance for them. When flowers grow tall, I usually like to see them in tall containers—sunflowers, delphinium for example. For flowers that grow in masses or have very heavy heads, you want deep containers with substance to balance their weight. Think what a lilac bush looks like and you will see what I mean. For little flowers with short stems you want low bowls and baskets. Knowing how flowers behave when cut, what they like, also helps in choosing containers. Some need a lot of water, some need very little. Some flowers are very stable; you place them and they stay as they are placed. Others bend and move— tulips even grow—in the vase. These need containers where they have space to move. Knowing a flower's habits also helps you decide how to arrange it. Tulips, for example, are very difficult to use in strict symmetrical designs.

A taste of the container possibilities to be found in kitchen cupboards: tin and copper molds, a tall glass bottle—for a single shapely dogwood branch or a three-foot stalk of rubrum lilies —crocks and bowls in several sizes, a brown-and-white bean pot—as handsome for jonquils as for the more expected calendulas or sunflowers—and a fat brass jar that without its cover would welcome a jaunty tuft of marigolds or black-eyed Susans.

They move too much. It's when you try to arrange flowers against their nature or against the shape of the container that you get into trouble."

Certain flowers at certain periods in history have been so popular that they inspired the creation of special containers. Seventeenth-century tulipières or tulip glasses are separate pottery containers, usually in graduated sizes, that stack one on top of another to make pyramids if the containers are square or triangular, balusters if they are bowl-shaped. Each container has three or four spouts in which the flowers are inserted. They display tulips handsomely—and some are beautiful objects in themselves. Vases that almost literally arrange the flowers you put in them were made in many periods and countries. The ancient Chinese and Persians had flask-shaped vases where the single long neck was replaced by a cluster of small ones—sometimes as many as nine—each meant to hold one or two flowers. These are usually called spout vases, a name also applied to a very different design—five or seven funnel-like vases joined to make a fan-shaped container—that was popular in France and England in the late eighteenth century. Other eighteenth-century creations are little blue-and-white bricks with perforated lids made to hold small, delicate flowers; bowls and urns and convoluted rococo containers, also with perforated tops, sometimes fixed, sometimes removable; and branching or pyramidal épergnes designed to hold combinations of fruit and flowers. Epergnes were also Victorian favorites; a characteristic one was a low crystal bowl for fruit or ferns and short-stemmed flowers surmounted by a tall crystal trumpet for long-stemmed roses or carnations. Antique examples of these "flower-arranging containers" are for the most part rare and hard to come by, but some of them can be found in well-executed contemporary reproductions. There are modern variations as well, generally composed of simple glass or metal tubes fastened together or held in some kind of frame. Many are very good-looking in their own right, and they simplify flower arranging by shaping the arrangement for you. But, just because they do, they are often less interesting to work with in the long run than a simpler container that gives more scope to your own imagination.

Half-hidden by a summery cloud of wild indigo, *baptisia tinctoria*, a big copper wash basin in the living-room window of a remodeled barn. This is a container that keeps its place in the sun year round. In the winter it is filled with pine cones and kindling for the nearby Franklin stove, which are replaced in spring by apple-blossom branches or lilacs. Summer fields supply a succession of bloom: Queen Anne's lace, butterfly weed, tiger lilies. In autumn, it may hold masses of starry Michaelmas daisies, or bronzy chrysanthemums, or an arrangement of rose-hips, bittersweet, and rich red sumach panicles.

About the colors and textures of containers for specific flowers there is little general advice to be offered. Color is so personal a matter and the possible combinations so endless. Flowers seem to adapt themselves equally happily to any surface, rough or smooth, and with a few exceptions to any container material. Gerbera and anemones dislike metal containers and wilt almost immediately in them. Roses, too, are affected by metals, but to a much smaller degree, and a slightly shortened life may be a small price to pay for the enhancement given them by a silver bowl.

The real problem with collecting containers to suit the flowers you like is that your likes seem to increase with each new flower you meet, and the containers soon overflow the space you have to keep them. A sensible point of view to take when storage space is limited is to select for maximum flexibility. With just a few containers you can create many effects. The key is simplicity—clean shapes, colors, and materials that do not compete with the flowers or with their environment. Bud vases are extremely versatile and a dozen of them take less room to store than a dozen wine glasses. They need not match but are more successful in formal designs when they do. For bouquets of medium-size flowers—tulips, daisies, gerbera, carnations, roses, lilies—Ronaldo likes clear glass fishbowl vases, about eight inches in diameter. Simple cubes in glass or ceramic are extremely useful both singly and arranged in multiples as centerpieces. Classic oriental bowl-shapes in small sizes are perfect for all kinds of small flowers—like violets, pinks, and garnet or sweetheart roses. Baskets come in almost any size or shape and are almost universally usable. These few suggestions by no means exhaust the possibilities.

Few of us end up making our choices from a single point of view. More likely you will have some containers for specific places, some for specific flowers, and some that are widely adaptable. But however large or flexible your collection, there comes a time when you look at your containers and nothing seems quite right. Perhaps you are given flowers you do not usually have, or you have an idea for an arrangement that demands something different. Take another look around the house. You may find just what you need in the kitchen—a pitcher, a casserole, a mold, a mixing bowl, a canister—or in the dining room—a goblet, a tankard, a cup or a mug, a tureen, a vegetable dish, a carafe or a decanter, a finger bowl, soup bowl, or sugar bowl. Almost every house has a store of possibilities, and objects need not even be good-looking to have potential. With the homeliest of household articles Ronaldo improvises delightful containers. An ordinary pail given a wrapping of straw or tatami can move right into the living room. A baking pan similarly dressed becomes a centerpiece. Covered with fabric or moss or leaves, plain plastic refrigerator bowls or boxes turn into decorative flower holders. Characteristically, Ronaldo improvises and invents containers as often to express an idea as to fill a need, and in some of his most original and enchanting creations arrangement and container are one and the same.

"I love to see flowers in the garden," he says, "so I make baskets of moss and branches to give them the environment of the garden, to bring the feeling of the whole garden indoors. It is a little more difficult than just arranging flowers, but you create something just for the flowers, for the movement you see in them."

These containers are not difficult to make—Ronaldo demonstrates how in Chapter 10—nor are the materials he uses difficult to get. The basic forms can be found around the house or in the supermarket, the leaves in the garden or at a flower shop; and if moss or tatami are not available locally they can be ordered by mail. Some sources are listed in the same chapter. The technique takes only a little practice to master, and once you get your hand in, you will start coming up with shapes and coverings of your own.

You may feel that making special containers is a step further than you wish to go in decorating with flowers, but once you focus your eye and imagination on the subject, you will never, in any season, be without attractive and interesting objects in which to arrange flowers. And in all of Ronaldo's creations there are ideas for presentation that can be adapted to containers you have or can find or recycle.

Two simple elements, a glass globe set on a hurricane cylinder, combine to make a striking container for a graceful arc of pink, white, and red cosmos. Glass globes with wide openings are among the most useful and flexible of flower containers—their clarity and simplicity adapt them to any kind of environment. In them, flowers scarcely need arranging, falling quite naturally into pleasing lines. These globes come in sizes to fit any flower from the smallest to the largest, but Ronaldo finds those that are about eight inches in diameter the most generally serviceable, either singly or combined to make more complex containers.

Pitchers in any size and shape take naturally to flower arrangements. Here, a white ironstone lemonade pitcher as country Victorian as the plump and parti-colored bouquet it holds. The summer garden mixture of petunias, foxgloves, verbenas, veronica, red and white flowering tobacco, zinnias, rambler roses, and platycodon crowned with a pair of yellow lilies, is laced with wildlings—milkweed, goldenrod, Queen Anne's lace, wheat, and timothy.

Charming containers for small-flower bouquets—none are taller than eight inches—that normally act other parts on the dining table or tea tray. Once you have seen the silver sugar-lump canister filled with forget-me-nots and primroses, or with red and pink geraniums, or white phlox, or violet petunias, or a tangle of bright red autumn berries, you may take it off its sugar diet permanently. The teapot takes well to fluffy flowers of the same sort. The two sweetmeat dishes are perfect for a low mound of gardenias or a single one floated. The trumpet-shaped goblet would hold a tight and formal nosegay or a loose handful of lily of the valley with equal aplomb. Tumblers and pitchers and punch-cups—footed like this one or flat-bottomed—are endlessly adaptable. For large flowers and bouquets on a grand scale, look for containers among the larger table accessories like wine coolers, ice buckets, punch bowls, salad bowls, and soup tureens.

A pair of open-back brass ducks are
given arching papyrus tails and are re-
feathered with roses, moss, and ruffly
galax leaves.

In a highly stylized autumn design one stalk of giant white lilies soars over a thicket of white statice. The container is the versatile glass globe made temporarily opaque and leopard spotted. Its slipcover is a napkin tied tightly with raffia, the loose ends spread in an ornamental pair of corollas—an imaginative but easy technique (which Ronaldo demonstrates in Chapter 10).

Glass globes paired on a dining table ▶ hold mixed bouquets of florist's spring-in-winter flowers—apricot tulips, yellow daffodils, freesia and forsythia, blue lace flowers, white lilies and narcissus and daisies. The sculptured candlestick and candlebearing vase-stands were created for Ronaldo by Brazilian artist Paulo Nobre. It is not difficult, however, to visualize these bouquets lighted by candleholders in any one of a variety of styles and materials.

Five glass globes compose a container that suits tulips to perfection. It gives them space to bend and move and arrange themselves into graceful designs. Poppies, ranunculus, or any flower that curves naturally would find it sympathetic. Filled with shorter-stemmed and fluffier flowers—a mixture of garden roses, hybrid teas, ramblers, floribundas, for example, or nothing but delicate maidenhair ferns—the container creates compositions of a different but equally attractive kind. Ronaldo glues the five bowls together with clear epoxy—a semipermanent arrangement. After a certain amount of washing, epoxy tends to lose its sticking power and has to be replaced, or it can be removed altogether, returning the bowls to their original roles as individual containers.

◄ Mounded with fluffy white carnations, a gourd container shares a table with an African basket and a vivacious Art Deco head. The gourd is another of Ronaldo's favorite containers-of-all-work. "For me it has a very strong appeal. The gourd is the first container given by nature to hold water, it goes back to the beginning of civilization, and it is very much of my country, Brazil. It is very primitive, very natural, very pure." The gourd is also a container that you can grow and dry for yourself, given the proper conditions, which are discussed in Chapter 10. It is, however, a container that has to be given some sort of stand or base—flat-sided gourds are an only occasional accident in nature.

◀ A two-tiered topiary of double orange day lilies in a gourd with a support system—three loops of rope tied to make a triangular knotted base—which would appeal to a macramé expert. The long-stemmed lilies—tied tightly with raffia, then spread apart with moss tucked between them and shaped into a ball—are held in position by crumpled chicken wire inside the gourd. For an informal arrangement of the same flowers in the same quantity, no wire would be needed.

A trio of gourds composed in a far from primitive setting. Each holds one tall dark-blue delphinium, one violet anemone, and one low cluster of starry white narcissus: three flower stems are about all its tiny opening will accept. The arrangement takes its lively rhythm from the natural curves of the flowers and the varying shapes and heights of the containers. Nature rarely provides identical gourds in any case, but their heights can be adjusted by the size and spread of their supporting dowel tripods.

Holding a green-and-white bouquet of galax leaves and freesia buds and blossoms, a small gourd sits on a tripod of thin wooden dowels. These are held together with raffia tied and wrapped in and out and round and round, then given a coat of clear lacquer. A simple support that somehow suggests the silver mountings made for coconut shells in the late Renaissance. In fact, a cleaned and polished coconut shell makes as attractive a container. With an electric saw it is easy enough to cut the top off cleanly; the only trick is getting out all the meat without cracking the shell.

33

Bouquets in kitchen containers composed in a kitchen still life. Multicolored zinnias, Queen Anne's lace, and yellow achillea fill two white-enameled metal pitchers. The mustard pot holds orange butterfly weed, pink everlasting pea, yellow achillea, and a dahlia bud in a ruff of galax leaves, and the yellow coffee mug holds a handful of lavender pansies. The exclamation point: a stalk of white powderpuff hollyhock blossoms in a flask that usually serves as a wine carafe.

A bouquet as innocent and spontaneous as a child's:
golden coreopsis, timothy grass, and galax leaves in a
gray stoneware jar. The recycled container entered the
household as packaging for mustard but has become
the household favorite for flowers. An agreeable shape
in an unrestricting color, it seems to suit almost any
flower, wild or garden grown, and lends itself to a
variety of arrangements, casual or carefully designed.

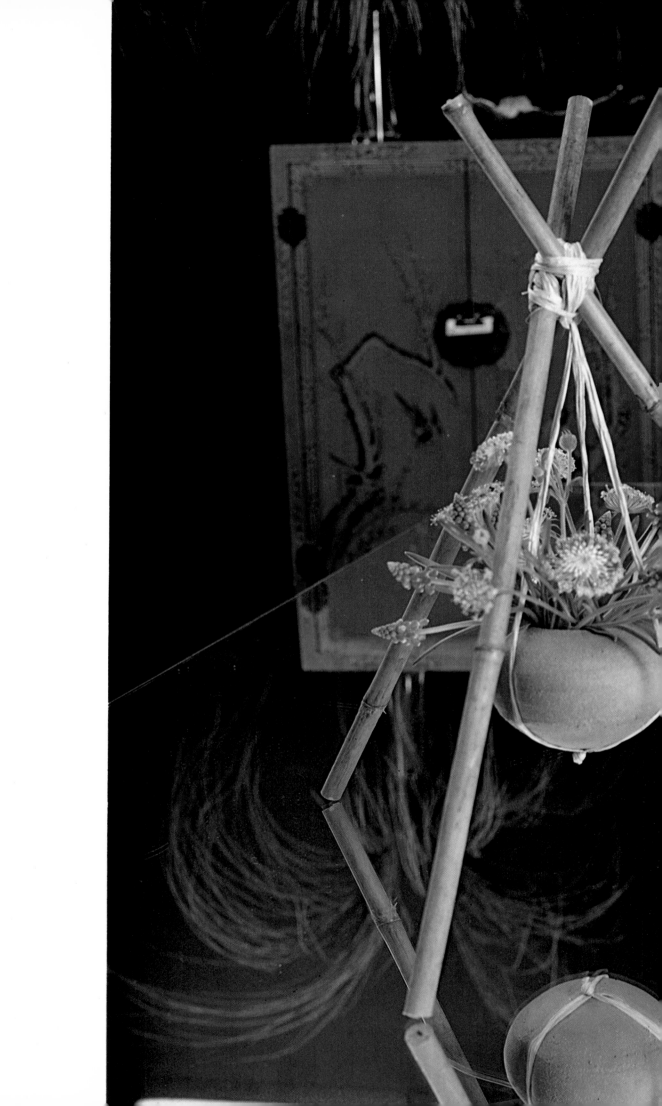

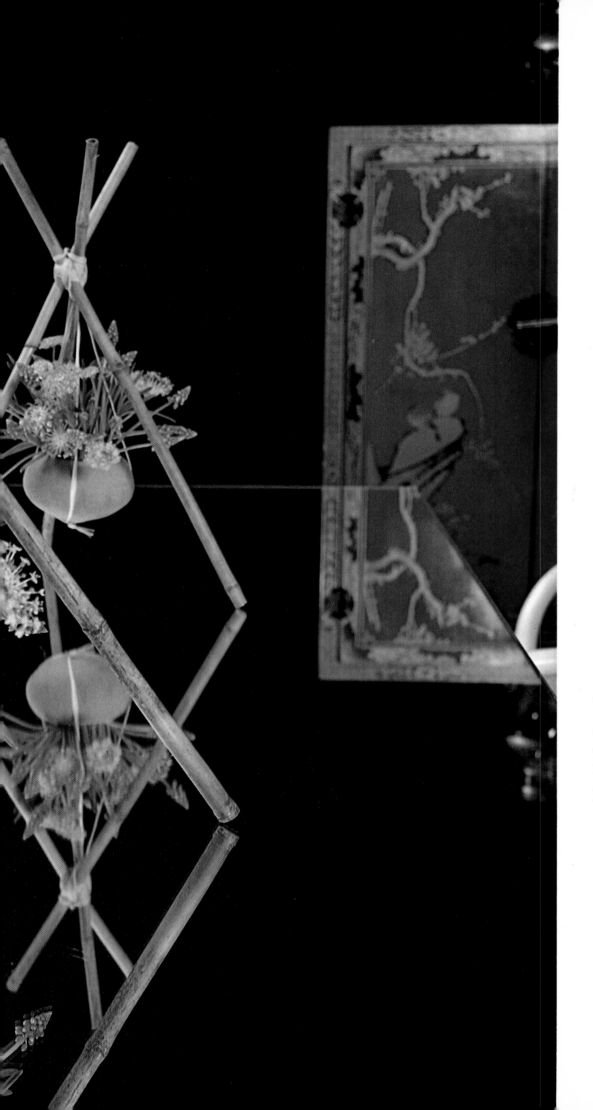

Terra-cotta pots of blue lace flowers and grape hyacinths swing from tall bamboo tripods—a whimsical suggestion of the campfire cauldron. A talent for improvising containers soon leads to the design of more permanent ones. The terra-cotta bowl is grooved to channel the raffia strands by which it is suspended.

◄ In a mossy branch-handled basket created to give them a bit of garden inside the house, sprightly little red-and-yellow Persian Carpet zinnias are arranged just as they grow, even to the sprigs of wild leafy spurge poking up among them. Ronaldo loves moss baskets. "They give such a strong sense of nature." He will make one out of anything that holds water—in this case a plastic basin—if it is the size and shape he wants. He shows exactly how the transformation is accomplished in Chapter 10.

A fantasy in moss and branches, more an ornament in itself than flower container. Branches and twigs are stuffed in a moss-covered jar and bent into an acorn finial, a classic topiary form. A few white freesias peek out from the tangle; half-hidden in it are tufts of aromatic gray oak moss.

Pink weigela and bleeding heart so entwined with their moss basket that arrangement and container become one. Weigela branches swoop over the handle and around the container; delicate sprays of bleeding heart spring from its center and climb the handle. The basket was an ordinary 46-ounce juice can.

Pink lilies and ranunculus, white freesia in a fabric-wrapped container that is one of Ronaldo's trademarks. He calls it a "kinkaju," and it is oriental in inspiration. "The Chinese and Japanese always wrap precious things in fabric." The kinkaju's precise folds depend upon a specially made double container, but it is not difficult to think of more casual ways of wrapping and tying containers to create a similar effect.

◄ Covered in blue-and-white batik to match the tablecloth, a kinkaju makes a delightful centerpiece. Flowers in it seem to float above the table. Here they are all white—roses, freesia, and lace flowers—and tucked between layers of galax leaves.

2. The Seasons of Spring

Amaryllis in moss-wrapped pots, each with its own enclosure like a unicorn in a tapestry. The little fences are constructed of neatly sawn lengths of quince branches, the uprights pushed into the earth around the bulb, the crossbars wrapped and tied to them with lengths of raffia. A moss covering gives a touch of the garden to any pot of forced bulbs; the fence frames most effectively those flowers that grow very tall, as amaryllis always and narcissus sometimes do. Also tapestry-like, the spray of lily of the valley tucked into one pot adds fragrance, as does the little bundle of aromatic oak moss tied to the fence rail.

To talk about decorating with spring flowers, it is important to specify which spring flowers we mean. Early narcissus and snowdrops call for very different treatment and contribute very different ornamental qualities than the later tulips and daffodils or the still later peonies and lilacs. The successive waves of spring flowers seem to grow brighter and bolder with the sun as it rises from the winter solstice to the annually shifting dividing line between spring and summer.

For flowers in the house the first season of spring is midwinter. Before Thanksgiving the first forced bulbs turn up in the florist shops: paperwhite narcissus, lilies of the valley, freesia—so tender it must be greenhouse grown in the northern states. And, even in an apartment, all you need is a little space and attention to surprise Christmas with a spring garden of home-forced narcissus, French-Roman hyacinths, lilies of the valley, or the little bulb irises, purple reticulata, and yellow danfordiae. Or, dramatic where these are delicate, the easiest bulb of all to flower in the house, amaryllis, in reality not a spring bulb but a summer one in its native South Africa. However, since it is a winter and spring flower in our houses, it is included in this chapter in the instructions for forcing bulbs on page 239.

A bowl or pot of narcissus has such associative appeal for us—in addition to its beauty—that it really need serve no decorative purpose beyond its own existence. Still, wrapping the pot in moss as Ronaldo does intensifies the illusion of a chunk of garden brought indoors. Amaryllis demands more careful placement in a room. The strong springing lines of the leaves and stem, the large and shapely flowers are most effective when the plant is placed and lighted as the piece of living sculpture it is. Unless, that is, you are prepared for the extravagance of displaying these dramatic flowers in quantity. A possible extravagance if you flower your own, and one that can be unforgettable: amaryllis in different shades of red and orange, about fifteen of them, massed like organ pipes in a deep window and seeming to grow out of the angel-wing begonias clustered in front of them. The same arrangement in a mixture solely of pinks and white would light up a room in a different but equally memorable way.

The true forced flowers of early spring—crocus, narcissus, French-Roman hyacinths, the little irises—are small, fragile, for the most part delicate in color, but with strong scents and distinct personalities. Little jewels to be treated as such. For convenience they are usually grown in flats or largish pots, but forced bulbs need not stay in the containers they grew up in. If they are gently handled, it does them no harm to be lifted out and separated. (When the roots are too enmeshed to come apart easily it is kinder to the plant to cut through the tangle rather than trying to pull it apart.)

Given the individual bulbs to work with, many interesting presentations are possible. One can display the whole plant—roots, bulb, and blossom—like a single flower. Carefully wash off the dirt, then balance the bulb in a tall glass cylinder or in one of the special vases designed for forcing hyacinths in water, always keeping the water level just below the base of the bulb. An acquaintance with old botanical prints will suggest how decorative this can be.

Ronaldo makes gardens with individual bulbs. A single crocus or hyacinth sprouting in an expanse of moss re-creates a slice of spring turf in the liner of a shallow basket. For a formal garden in miniature, white Dutch hyacinths circle precisely around a central cluster of white narcissus in moss-covered sand in a fourteen-inch terra-cotta pot saucer. A fantasy woodland in a moss basket mixes cut and growing flowers. None of these little gardens needs a container more than two or three inches deep. The larger pot saucers, plain or moss-wrapped, do very well, but if you look around the kitchen you will find many other choices—low vegetable dishes, porcelain or enamel baking dishes, and, given a covering of moss, even cake and pie tins. Whether your garden is large or small, round or rectangular, depends on the size and shape of the table it is planned for. A practical note: if there is any chance of moisture from the container damaging the table surface—always a problem with unglazed terra cotta—the table should be protected with a piece of clear plastic film under

A fresh-from-the-garden Easter basket tied with a flowing raffia bow makes a velvety green nest for the smooth white eggs and cheery sprigs of blue lace flower and white and yellow freesia.

A fantasy of the beginning of spring gathers grape hyacinths, lilies of the valley, and blue lace flowers in a moss basket under and around crossed arches of bare branches—like small flowers growing in the middle of the forest. A fantasy inspired for Ronaldo by "the way the vines come down from the trees in Brazil. The vines are so thick and the air is so humid that they have flowers growing on them as well as under them. I wanted to create the same kind of environment, a circle of life that goes from earth up and back to earth again."

the arrangement. Cut to the shape of the container, the plastic is nearly invisible.

When spring really comes to the garden, there is even more material for making table-top landscapes. As long as they have not been planted too deep, small bulbs can be safely lifted, roots and all, and brought indoors to give a week's pleasure—far longer than if they were cut—and then returned to their natural habitat. Snowdrops, crocus, scillas, grape hyacinth, miniature daffodils are a few of the possibilities which are not confined to bulbs. Many other delicate spring plants are equally appealing treated this way. One of the loveliest lunch tables I have ever seen, set with green-sprigged china on an apple-green organdy cloth, had as a centerpiece a bed of pale blue violets growing in a glass-lined silver vegetable dish.

Even when they are cut, Ronaldo often arranges small spring flowers in miniature landscapes. Narcissus, hyacinths, freesia, lilies of the valley, lace flowers, Star of Bethlehem or the equally star-like Neapolitan alliums in any combination seem to grow from a carpet of moss that conceals the water-absorbent plastic foam holding their tender stems in position. With the same flowers he also makes casual little mixed bouquets such as a child might gather and places them singly or in multiples to refresh a collection of objects or a table setting with their delicious scents and delicate colors.

Later in the spring come the larger and showier tulips, jonquils, daffodils. These Ronaldo rarely mixes, either with each other or with other flowers. Whether the arrangement is loose and casual, taking its form from the natural movement of the flowers, or a carefully shaped mass of blossoms, the flowers are all of a kind and usually all of a color as well.

"So often the inspiration for arranging a flower comes from the way you see it growing in the garden. I always see tulips or daffodils planted in blocks or sweeps of color and I like to see them that way in the house."

Tulips and daffodils are not self-effacing flowers. Even in soft colors and relatively small quantities they attract the eye instantly in a room. When they are all of a color the attraction is intensified, and even more so if the

45

Airy clusters of paperwhite narcissus garland a spring table. Giving each bulb its own moss-filled pot and saucer emphasizes the slender grace of the single plant and makes it easy to arrange the plants attractively on a table of any shape or size. It took just one big pot of bulbs, gently separated and repotted, to decorate this white marble table.

color is brilliant. Therefore their placement in a room depends on where you want attention focused. As a general guideline, masses of color and strong shapes are more effective if used sparingly. Three dozen tulips massed have far more decorative impact than three bowls of a dozen tulips each dotted around a room. Arrangements that cannot help saying "Look at me!" tend in multiples to distract instead of decorate. In this they are unlike single flowers, which quietly complement their little individual environments.

Trees and shrubs give another spring-long succession of flowers for the house. The first forced branches of flowering quince arrive at the florist's with the first midwinter bulbs. As soon as you see buds swelling on branches in late winter or early spring, you can cut in your garden and force forsythia, pussy willow, dogwood, spirea, and almost all of the fruit trees and their purely ornamental cousins like flowering quince and cherry. It is even easier than forcing bulbs (the procedure is explained in detail on page 238). As long as you do not put them in bright sunlight, you can even arrange your branches as soon as cut and enjoy the whole flower-unfolding process. If you are not concerned about speeding up spring, cut just as the buds are about to open outdoors. Restrained cutting that respects the form of growth will not hurt and in many cases is a positive benefit to trees and shrubs. Forsythia, quince, spirea, lilac, mock orange among others are strengthened. They have to be pruned anyway as soon as the flowers fade.

With most flowering branches it is the quality of line and not the quantity of branches that counts, whether you buy or cut them. One or two well-shaped branches are far more decorative than a tangle. For small arrangements a few sprigs or the tip of a branch may be all that is needed. And whether you buy or cut, you may have to do some additional pruning to make nature conform to your ideas of a well-shaped branch.

There is another way nature needs editing, and not just for decorative reasons: most, if not all, of the leaves should be removed from flowering branches to be used in arrangements. The blossoms show to greater advantage and they last much longer when they do not have to compete with

Yellow, orange, and white freesia in a Chinese lacquered basket. The flowers' natural curves are an especially happy choice for the basket's spiraling construction, and they are arranged in a very easy way. "You pick the flowers, bunch them in your hand, cut all the stems right across the same length and put them in the vase, letting them fall in easily from your hand. There is no technique, the design comes from the movement of the flowers themselves. The only skill is judging the right number of flowers for the container, not too many, not too few." Ronaldo's no-technique technique can be used to make appealing informal bouquets, mixed or all of a kind, with most flowers — very large, very fragile, or stiff-stemmed ones excepted.

A whole bed of tulips for the table left in the flat in which they were forced. The rustic wrapping of moss and hay is simply stapled to the wooden flat — with such shaggy materials the staples do not show. A spectacular sweep of color for a centerpiece or a coffee table, but one that takes some advance planning — the autumn before you need it if you plant a flat and grow it yourself — which takes space and preferably a cold frame — and reasonable warning if your florist must order it for you from a grower. However, you can create a very good duplicate with cut tulips by massing them tightly in a rectangular container packed with water-absorbent plastic foam.

50

leaves for their water. If you want more than a few leaves for design reasons, it is better to cut and condition separate sprays of leaves. Of course, this problem does not arise when in nature the flowers appear before the leaves, as happens with magnolia and with varieties suggested for forcing.

Simple compositions of branches alone or with only one or two added flowers provide a welcome change of pace. "Sometimes you want space and lines and not masses. The way you use flowers, even in the same locations in the house, should change just as the flowers change with the seasons."

Not all the flowering shrubs and trees are linear in character. It is hard to think of lilacs or rhododendrons except as masses of color. And these Ronaldo composes in masses. Not necessarily large ones, perhaps just a few fluffy rhododendron clusters with enough leaves left to give a sense of the separate flower heads. Lilacs and anemones are a favorite combination. So are lilacs and peonies, a classic that offers a whole gamut of possible compositions in white, pink, red, and lavender. Lilacs and peonies are also classic ingredients for large and lavish mixtures, bouquets on a grand scale for grand spaces—churches, museums, ballrooms, lobbies—and, once in a while, for a party mood at home.

"When you want abundance—masses that are really masses, splashing and tumbling down—you use the flowers as a painter uses brush strokes. You build your composition with the different shapes, the different textures. They are the essentials. You can use many colors or only one."

For a quantity of flowers Ronaldo's preferred container is large, holds a quantity of water, and has a wide mouth. "The diameter of the vase should be at least half the diameter of the arrangement. Then you don't force or squeeze the stems. They can go right down into the water and they hold each other in place—you don't need wire to hold them."

That flowers share this preference they show by lasting longer, always provided the water is regularly replenished. However, as often as not the large arrangement must be made in a less capacious container, particularly when it must be placed at or above eye level in order to count in a room full

Full-blown garden tulips assembled in a little indoor garden. Their plot of earth is a square baking tin packed with water-filled foam, carpeted with moss, and banded with a strip of tatami. For support, the flowers are tied with raffia to three stair-stepped quince-branch fences. The very cultivated "weed" in this orderly garden is blue centaurea.

Lilies of the valley display an unaccustomed formality in
a pair of tiny trumpet-shaped vases placed to frame a
collection of boxes stacked in a Biedermeier étagère.

A sprig of white azalea and two of yellow freesia tied with moss and raffia into a lighthearted arabesque for a long-necked Chinese porcelain vase. The shape comes naturally from the contrasting curves of the stems. The colors are chosen to suit the container.

A miscellany of spring flowers divided into little nosegays for one of Ronaldo's composed containers—five one-glass wine carafes epoxied together. The minuscule white starbursts mixed with the larger star of Bethlehem, freesia, and lily of the valley are Queen Anne's lace, a summer weed which, in a rather belated tribute to its beauty, is now being grown commercially year round. All through spring the garden produces little flowers to gather in bouquets: snowdrops, crocuses, scillas, miniature daffodils, grape hyacinths, primroses, chionodoxas, wild cyclamen, fritillarias, lady tulips, blue or white violets, forget-me-nots, coral bells, columbines, bleeding heart. Small and delicate, they bring a touch of the season's scent and color to a tea or breakfast tray, a bedside or an end table, a desk or a shelf.

of people. Then Ronaldo uses crushed chicken wire to keep the flowers in position. It is wired, taped, or tied to the container. Longevity is of necessity curtailed, but single flowers can be removed as they fade (and replaced if desired) to help the bouquet last for a period of time. If the reason for its splendid existence really ends when the party is over, it is worth considering that the flowers may give equal and longer pleasure rearranged in smaller bouquets for several rooms.

The interplay of the forms and textures of many different kinds of flowers gives the great traditional mixed bouquet its interest and vitality. It sometimes happens, particularly in spring, that just when there is an occasion that calls for a big bouquet the garden cannot supply all the variety you need. Ronaldo has found that to get a color or shape or texture he wants he can supplement the flowers of spring with the seasonless flowers of the market—stock, snapdragon, or delphinium—without losing the mood of the season. It is the total effect that counts, not the individual brush strokes. And when you are caught by the beauty of a bouquet you do not stop to think whether the flowers come from garden, shop, or greenhouse, or to precisely what season they belong. In fact, seasons themselves are not precise. Flowers bloom earlier or later in different parts of the country and even in the same garden from year to year. Early roses may or may not join the last lilacs and tulips, but, barring a truly disastrous spell of weather, many summer stand-bys are already in flower before the end of May. Raw materials for arranging seem to increase in quantity and variety every day as the sun warms up and stays longer. The last season of spring is also the first taste of summer's abundance.

Orange and white ranunculus bunched by color in a pair of goblet-like vases placed away from the center of a round table. It is a more pleasant arrangement for diners than a single bouquet centered would be when the flowers, as here, are at eye level. As long as you keep sight lines clear it is possible to deviate comfortably from the general rule that flowers for dining should be above or below eye level. Massing instead of mixing the colors somehow seems to give extra snap and freshness to a series of small bouquets. Imagine, for example, a long table with a line of ranunculus in pink, orange, yellow, and white, arranged color by color like the pair shown here.

Nature did most of the arranging in what seems a formal composition in a black marble urn, a design that takes several hours to make because nature needs time to do her work. In the beginning only the cut and conditioned grape hyacinths are placed in the container, which is filled with water-saturated foam to hold them in position. At first their stems are straight, but at the end of an hour or two the weight of their heads bends them naturally into flowing curves. Once they have arranged themselves, lilies of the valley and two tall stems of delphinium buds are added to finish the composition. The budded stems and leaves of Virginia cowslips or bleeding heart are perfect spring garden replacements for the seasonless florist's delphinium. Many flowers with heavy heads and tender stems will move and bend in the vase — tulips are also adept at this — a trick an arranger can, with a little patience, use to great advantage.

Orange and white ranunculus in an arrangement that suggests a giant flower with the green glass vase as calyx, the individual blossoms as petals. Each flower is cut and placed individually — ranunculus is fragile and bruises or shatters unless carefully handled — but no wire or foam is used to hold the stems; they hold each other in place. You build the shape starting at the bottom and working up, turning the vase from time to time as you fill in flowers to keep it balanced in the round, and finishing off — again at the lower edge — with a few longer out-and-downward-curving stems. Ronaldo likes to arrange ranunculus, like tulips and daffodils, in lightly controlled all-of-a-kind masses that give a room a splash of color while respecting and showing off the natural movement and form of the flowers.

A handful of white ranunculus and a few stems of white
freesia casually gathered in a slender pewter-mounted
pitcher: a very simple arrangement that transforms its
kitchen-counter setting. The cut onion is an irresistible
addition to complete the still life.

Small in relation to the objects around it, one bunch of tulips, simply arranged, lights up its whole environment. The red-and-yellow-striped tulips pick up the gold and bronze in Frederick Wehmer's painting; white ones would intensify the silver.

A blue-and-white bouquet of imposing size but free and airy character, composed with a florist's mix of spring and summer flowers: dogwood, iris, delphinium, stock. To build his design, Ronaldo first places the dogwood branches. Then, beginning at the lower edge and working up and into the center, he adds the softer flowers, grouping them for contrasts of color and shape. As more and more flowers are added the stems hold each other in position — no chicken wire is needed. The wide-mouthed Mexican terra-cotta jar, however, needs a liner — in this case a snug-fitting plastic tub — because it is unglazed and hence porous. Another practical note: Any large arrangement like this should be made in the place it is to decorate.

A pair of bold bouquets in shapes and textures of white — dogwood, iris, stock, and Shasta daisies. The dozen blue irises are so pale they count as cool white in the total scheme. These are bouquets designed to dress a living room for a big party, and they are all that is needed to do it. Because the containers — flat urns that are part of the room's permanent decoration — are rather small in relation to the mass of flowers, the flowers need extra support, given by filling the urns with crumpled chicken wire securely taped to their rims. The tape is concealed by the fan of broad green Ti leaves that softens and rounds off the lower edge of the arrangement. These flowers are sturdy ones, but even they will last longer if a bouquet in such a container is considered as an ornament for a night, then broken up and rearranged.

Soft flowers set off by the clean lines and sleek surfaces of their setting, anemones are scattered like scarlet stars through a single fluffy but carefully formed mass of white lilac in a black marble mantelpiece urn.

Sweet william in a seed-catalogue array of white and pinks and reds and stripes collected to ornament a cocktail table. Each color is tied separately in a tight galax-collared bunch—just like the nosegays that fill the baskets of Parisian flower-vendors—then all the bunches are piled in a moss-covered bowl. A fresh and charming way to fix flowers for a party—and at the end of the evening you have a nosegay to offer each departing guest.

An armload of lilacs—sprays of leaves, sprays of white and purple blossoms—and a dozen red anemones swirled together in a large white pottery plant tub. The lively rhythm of the design is an orchestration of the natural movement of the flowers. It makes a big and glowing decoration for a table between meals, or an equally splendid one for a fireplace or a tall window.

Mushrooms and lace flowers, a surprising but delightful combination of smooth and lacy circles of white. The container is a baking tin filled with water-saturated foam, its slipcover a strip of tatami tied around with raffia. Toothpicks secure the mushrooms. It is an arrangement just for a day, but a very easy one to make, and the mushrooms will have another life in the cooking pot, the lace flowers in a vase.

65

3. The Magic of One Flower

A single lemon-yellow lily at the foot of a Chinese jar turned lamp base. It is at once a touch of life and color, and a piece of natural architecture as remarkable as the miniature silver pagoda beside it.

A flower arrangement that is just one flower—the idea shocks by its very simplicity. But how often, even when you are arranging flowers, do you really take the time to enjoy each individual blossom in all its intricate detail? Isolating a single flower, a single spray in its own vase focuses your eye on the beauty of its shape, color, texture, on the rhythms of its growth and structure. Once you have discovered the visual delights in even the simplest flower, Ronaldo's point of view seems completely natural.

"Truly to see and enjoy a flower, you must see it alone. When you love someone or something, you isolate them from the crowd, you see only the one. If I have ten flowers in my house there are ten places that have one flower rather than ten in one vase. For living with flowers I find it nicer to see them separately, to have a flower everywhere I look."

You can give your single flowers better care, too, and so they will last longer. When each is in its own vase, you can recut the stems and change the water every day—which would be impossible with a bouquet, for to recut and change water you really have to remake an arrangement. Most of us do not have time to do this every day.

Of course, there may be spaces in a room where you do need splashes of color, where the bulk of an arrangement is necessary. A single flower treated as a work of art brings something different to a room than an arrangement does. It is a touch of life and color you do not always notice at first glance, but when you do see it there is the added charm of discovery. Possibilities for placement are endless. Finding just the right spot depends on the flower you have and the things in a room. Perhaps a single speckled rubrum lily is perfect next to your celadon plate, but a single daisy feels more at home with the collection of Battersea boxes. And a single pink zinnia, placed on the kitchen counter, will bring the copper pots to life. With each flower comes a happy chance to create a new little still life and to see your rooms and your cherished objects with a fresh eye.

Each season, each month of the year brings a new crop of flowers to get acquainted with, to try in different places, or to give a sense of the year's

A composition in line with the strong simplicity of a Japanese brushstroke: one forked spring branch of flowering quince in the same basket of slender logs. The glass container set on a bed of moss practically disappears. To get just the right rhythm of flower and branch you may find you have to remove some flowers and twigs from your chosen branch. Wherever you place it in a room, this kind of arrangement needs space around it.

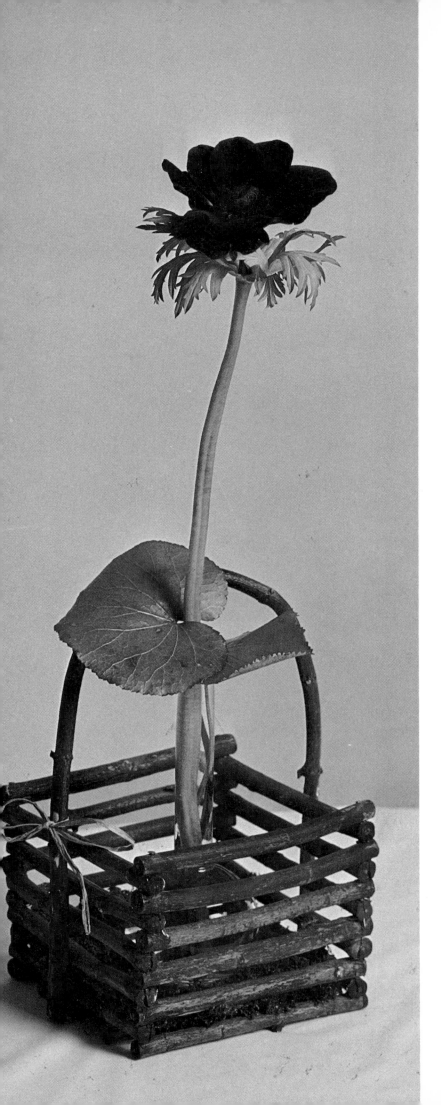

A single anemone in a clear glass flask, set in a basket built of bark-covered branches. The galax leaves echo the shape of the petals and connect the flower to the handle of its basket frame.

A gathering of tiny Staffordshire dogs, each in the shade of his own single flower, assembled for the entertainment of a lunch party. The flowers are a florist's mix of spring and summer—freesia, alstroemeria, star of Bethlehem, white lace flower, red painted daisies, red and white roses, and a big white Shasta daisy, all collared with galax leaves. The flowers can be changed—zinnias, nasturtiums, baby dahlias, phlox, pansies, pinks only begin a list of summer choices—but they should be short-stemmed and stay close to their china companions. Single flowers and collections make marvelous raw material for table decorations, formal or informal and in any mood that suits the character of the collection.

In a variation of vase within vase, tiny bottles hold a ranunculus bud, an anemone, a freesia, a tulip. An arrangement that takes just four flowers and would be a perfect centerpiece for a round glass or marble table, holding a fresh and different combination of flowers every week in the year.

A vase inside of a vase increases the stature of a single pink tulip in a collar of galax. A layer of shiny black pebbles conceals all but the neck of the bud vase that really holds the stem. In a hot or dry room, water to the pebble line in the outer vase will give the flower its own moist, preserving atmosphere.

passage to one chosen space. Using only the flower shop as a resource, the pink rubrum lily—returning to the previous example—might be succeeded later in the autumn by a spider chrysanthemum in mauve or white, followed by a crimson-and-gold Rothschild lily and, at Christmas, a scarlet camellia or a red-and-white striped one; in the spring by a yellow or blue or white Dutch iris, a green-touched fringed parrot tulip, a pink peony; then one by one all the roses of summer.

Given a garden, you have not only flowers to work with. Branches and buds, leaves and berries and even grasses lend themselves to this kind of arrangement. At their thinnest periods most gardens have something to offer when you are looking not for quantity but for a single note to complement a specific small environment: a well-shaped branch of forsythia before spring has really taken hold or an equally well-shaped one of greeny-gold maple in the fall, or clusters of bright red berries—barberry or cotoneaster—rescued from the snow.

A secondary blessing of single flowers is that you can enjoy colors or flowers that in mass might overpower—or be overpowered by—the decoration of your room. A big bouquet of marigolds could be a bit strident in a scheme of delicate pastels, one yellow marigold is a piquant zest. Conversely, in trying out single flowers, you may find unpredictable happy consonances that lead to successful combinations on a larger scale.

In spite of the simplicity of the basic idea, there is true artistry in the way Ronaldo presents a single flower. As a guiding principle in these as in all his arrangements, flowers are used in the same position as they grow. Hyacinths that stand straight in the garden stand straight in the vase. When flowers trail or bend in nature—nasturtiums or clematis, for example—they are allowed to follow their natural bent in arrangement. Each presentation is finally determined by the character of the particular flower and of the container, but there is one especially characteristic technique that Ronaldo uses again and again: a collar of galax leaves at the neck of the container from which the flower springs.

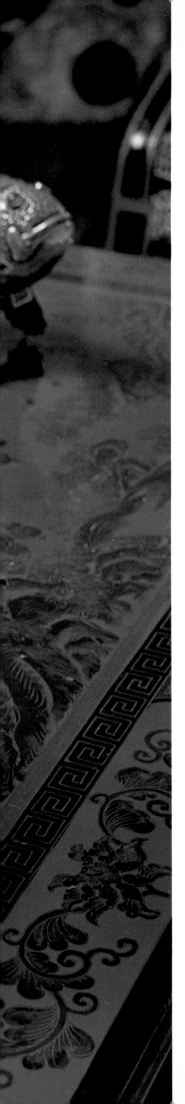

One purple anemone is tripled by a mirrored screen behind the eighteenth-century French marble and gilt-bronze clock. The tiny pottery vase has a tuft of moss in its mouth to hold the flower upright.

◄ Circled by a pair of articulated silver fish, a single stalk of Enchantment lilies in a crystal flask is enclosed in an eighteen-inch crystal globe. A simple, inventive design that makes a striking decoration at any season. Between the garden and the florist there is scarcely a week in the year that one or another variety of true lilies or day lilies is not available.

"Flowers usually grow between leaves, and leaves break the line of the vase. The vase stops at the leaves and from there up are the flowers. When I don't feel a relation between the vase and flower, I separate them. When the line of the vase and the line of the flower are the same, I don't. If I don't want leaves and the neck of the container is too big to hold the flower upright, I tuck a little bit of moss around it to support the stem—like a little bit of earth. Why do I use galax leaves so much? I like the shape, and I always visualize them growing wild in the Carolinas, a glossy carpet covering the ground with flowers pushing up through it."

Using the flowers' own leaves would seem the most natural way to "anchor" them to the earth. But even when you can pick them in the garden it does not always work. Some combinations are very successful— carnations with their own blue-cast and curling foliage or peonies with their distinctive leaves. For some flowers, however, cutting leaves irreparably damages the plant. Columbine falls into this category. Fortunately, for columbine you can grow hardy meadow rue to supply leaves that are almost identical. Some leaves are very soft, wilting or rotting quickly in contact with water and shortening the life of the flower. Daisies, chrysanthemums, and zinnias are examples that come immediately to mind. Still other leaves may be too stiff or too small, or, like agapanthus, too large for the single flower. And if you buy commercially grown flowers from a florist you know how often you get no leaves at all. As useful universal leaves, Ronaldo's favorite galax have more than their looks to recommend them. They are extremely long-lasting, in or out of an arrangement. A bunch of galax, in a glass of water or wrapped in damp paper, will keep almost indefinitely in the refrigerator. They are very easy to come by; most florists carry them or can order a supply for you. But there are other possibilities to consider—a ruff of small ferns, for example, or geranium leaves, either the very galax-like plain ones or the lacier rose- or lemon-scented varieties.

The single flower in its vase also serves Ronaldo as the starting point for more complex designs. Sometimes he places the vase in a basket or a

One stalk of flowers in a vase is not necessarily a simple design. Here agapanthus and nerine—from the garden in summer, the florist in winter—are presented in a highly personal way. For Ronaldo, "these flowers seem to lose contact with the earth, so I bring the earth— moss—up to them. It makes a pillow for the flower." Moss is tucked between each bud on the agapanthus umbrel and tied at the base of the nerine cluster—a styli- zation in the mood of the Chinese perfume bottles and carved mon- key that share the table.

clear glass bowl of polished pebbles or encloses it in a larger container—a fishbowl or a hurricane cylinder. Set in its own environment, its "frame," the single flower becomes a self-contained decoration—witty, charming, dramatic, or all three together. Ronaldo makes many arrangements by multiplication, with the single flower as building block. Two, three, or four containers on a tray, each different or all the same, with each flower different or all the same; a dozen flowers in a circle in the center of one table or dotted the length of another, grouped informally on a console or lined up in front of the window. On one fireplace with a collection of very early Oriental and Pre-Columbian figures, he uses bud vases with ferns that swoop around the figures and just one flower in each—perhaps gerbera—shooting out of the leaves.

With rather a small number of single flowers you can suggest a much larger arrangement. For example, stalks of delphinium, say seven, lined up like a hedge across the back of a summer buffet table and, in front of them, a line of smaller flowers, perhaps cosmos or poppies, give the whole table the feeling of a herbaceous border. Some of Ronaldo's formal designs with single flowers do require having a sufficient number of identical vases, but given the proper containers, they are a marvelous way to get maximum decoration with a minimum of material. This fresh and simple approach to living and decorating with flowers requires no special knowledge or technique, just a little imagination and a love of flowers.

A flock of little summer flowers perches on a wall-hung collection of miniatures, among them chairs, chains, and candle snuffers. In the thumb-size vases are zinnias, nasturtiums, stokesia, and a foxglove tip from the garden, freesia from the florist. Almost any small and colorful flowers would work—whatever you can find in the garden or have left from a larger arrangement. The wit of the composition depends on the play of scale between flower and object.

In this arrangement for four spring flowers — two freesia, a deep red ranunculus, and a rose-colored rose — the individual crystal flasks are firmly tied with raffia to a reed-and-bamboo tray. It is an easy and decorative stabilizing technique to use with baskets or any openwork container. For each vase two lengths of raffia were carried under the reeding, brought up to the base of the neck, tied, then wrapped round and round and knotted.

Four small containers — bud vases in slightly different shapes — are assembled to make a larger one, and attached for stability with clear epoxy to a square glass plate. Equally graceful summer replacements for the spring tulips: poppies, lilies, garden roses; winter ones: daisies, anemones, gerbera.

Tiny scarlet orchids in an antique
Chinese vase. Flower and container
seem made for each other, with the orchid leaves echoing the leaf pattern on
the porcelain. Anchored in the vase
with moss, the stems of the orchid, an
epidendrum, are lightly tied together in
airy curves with raffia bows. Raffia, soft
and lightweight, does not cut the stems
as wire might. A natural material, it is
visually a natural part of the design.

A pair of deep pink tigridia leaves and
blossoms, one just opening, spring
from a bulb-like blue ceramic vase. The
neck of the vase is packed with bits of
moss and tied with a whimsical raffia
bow. A spectacular but short-lived
summer flower even in the garden, tigridia is not very satisfactory for large
arrangements. In a single or double
flower arrangement longevity matters
less. For similar butterfly charm and the
same presentation, you might consider
a day lily or one of the more delicate
irises like *I. siberica, I. spuria,* or *I.
pseudacorus.* Or the graceful true dwarf
gladiolus, *G. nana,* not to be confused
with the stiff miniature size of the familiar standard variety.

Spring ranunculus and freesia add a living collection to the personal miscellany on a collector's bookshelf. With more than one blossom in a vase it is not strictly a single-flower arrangement, but the effect is the same—proof of the principle's flexibility. A year-long succession of flowers in the same reds, yellows, and oranges and with graceful curves to echo the swirling lines of the Art Nouveau luster plate might include in summer nasturtiums, poppies, cosmos, deep-red flowering tobacco; in autumn goldenrod, montbretia, geums, little dahlias; in winter yellow and orange alstroemeria, red anemones, or for a change of pace a single spray of white butterfly orchids.

82

A complement to their setting, but scarcely an unobtrusive one, these two giant white autumn lilies suggest that the role of the single flower in a tablescape has a great deal to do with the size of the flower. Each flower stands in a crystal wine carafe and is wedged upright with moss. The casually tied napkins balance the visual weight of the blossoms. The painting is by Frederick Wehmer.

Three lively stems of blue lace ▶ flower pull into one animated still life a Thai bronze Buddha and a small feather-hung fantasy table by Brazilian artist Paulo Nobre. Lace flower, or *Didiscus,* is a mid-summer bloomer in the garden, a year-round one at the florist. Its strong natural movement is used to decorative advantage by giving each stem a separate vase.

The essence of summer in a handful of flowers lined up on a window sill—a stalk of pink milkweed, a few sprigs of diminutive purple vetch, two sprays of blue veronica sharing a vase with a trail of shocking pink everlasting pea, two chive blossoms and a galax leaf, and, finally, one pink monarda. The chive and veronica are garden grown, as is the monarda, a cultivated form of an American wild flower with many aliases, among them bee balm and Oswego tea. All the rest are wildlings.

For a round table a circle of single flowers doubled; one
tall branching spray of freesia and one short-stemmed
ranunculus in each galax-collared vase. A very small
number of flowers—just ten—makes a very substantial
centerpiece.

4. The Riches of Summer

One berried twig of honeysuckle, one sprig of timothy, two blue and two white veronica, two white wild yarrow, three stems of white platycodon, a trailing spray of carrot leaves in a mustard jar. Just a few simple materials in a composition to inspire a seventeenth-century flower painter. For Ronaldo, such an arrangement "begins with an impulse. You have a flower and you visualize it in a certain position, then you build the design around that flower."

From June through September it seems as if nature had mobilized all her resources for the special benefit of the designer in flowers. A summer garden can be planted to produce any colors, any textures, any shapes, and in any combination. The biggest problem is choosing among all the shrubs and vines, annuals and perennials available. True, there are some limitations. The size of the garden, the kind of soil, the amount of sun and shade and water, the length of the growing season will all help to narrow down the selection. But taking these into consideration, you can still assemble in a garden the materials for any decorative effect you care to create, bold or subtle, large or small. The possibilities are so numerous that any suggestions are purely a matter of personal preference. I will make only one: Experiment. Try one or two new plants each year. A different color or shape or line is a great spur to the imagination. Plant and seed catalogues have pages full of unfamiliar and enticing flowers to try—most catalogues have some system for indicating which ones are good for cutting—and careful examination of the wares at a local nursery or garden shop will often uncover unexpected treasures.

Growing your own flowers—a pleasure in itself—gives you both a wider and more personal choice and an understanding of their habits that is extremely helpful when you come to creating designs with them. In Ronaldo's experience flowers are harder to work with when you do not know the plant and have only seen them cut, especially the less familiar ones. "If you can study flowers and think how they grow when you place them in a container, they will almost arrange themselves."

Very familiar flowers are what you have to choose from when you are gardenless and must depend on flower shops and roadside stands. Commercial growers tend to stick to strong, easily grown bread-and-butter varieties: calendulas, cornflowers, cosmos, dahlias, daisies, delphinium, gladiolus, larkspur, lilies, marigolds, snapdragons, stock, and zinnias, plus the always available roses, carnations, and chrysanthemums. Still, this is a summer list of considerable scope—within it you can find almost any

A silver ice tub filled to overflowing with summer flowers. For all its opulence the bouquet combines so many different kinds of blossoms that no one plant would miss its contribution. The collection comes half from the garden — white phlox, blue veronica, bright and dark red dahlias, pink rambler roses, pink and red-orange tearoses — and half from the wild — orange butterfly weed, pale pink bouncing bet and hot pink everlasting pea, goldenrod, white Queen Anne's lace, and wild camomile. With so many flowers, no wire or foam is needed to hold them in position, and the arrangement is built from the bottom up.

A fluffy mosaic of bright and white flowers in a blue stoneware crock: red, pink, and orange zinnias, dahlias in the same shades plus a creamy double one, white platycodon bells, sprigs of violet-blue perennial sage, wild white yarrow and its civilized cousin, achillea Coronation Gold. The tiny daisies sprinkled through are a common weed, one of the wild camomiles, which seems to have a different common name in every place it grows.

Two leafy sprays of lavender wisteria almost completely mask their slender Chinese bronze container and curl around a Cambodian deity. The slim column from which they seem to trail is seven tall stems of timothy grass tied together, their cattail heads held apart with moss to create a capital. A whimsical allusion to wisteria's need for something to cling to, and an imaginative use of a plant, timothy, so common that its decorative possibilities are almost never noticed.

Delicate stems of blue flax and snow-in-summer spray up and out from the center of a basket wrapped, handle and all, in moss. The flowers' natural curves echo the shape of the basket, whose velvety covering at the same time sets off their fragility and gives substance to the design. In such a precise arrangement, thin-stemmed flowers like these need water-saturated foam to support them.

color you need. And every year some surprises do turn up in the market to add zest to the basics.

Recently—a trend that deserves encouragement—florists have been selling garden flowers grown in pots for the house: forget-me-nots, flowering tobacco, geums, morning glories, lilies, cosmos, even zinnias. They are particularly effective clustered into little gardens in front of a window, either on the floor or on a broad sill; but one pot alone is enough to refresh a collection of indoor foliage plants. Even easier to come by in the city are the materials for tabletop gardens in the manner of the spring ones we have talked about. Especially in the early summer almost every flower shop has flats or boxes of pansies, alyssum, ageratum, dwarf marigolds, and the other small flowers intended for window-box or terrace planting, but with all kinds of potential for indoor decoration. Ageratum massed in moss-wrapped baking tins makes a spectacular carpet of blue for the center of a long dining table. Equally appealing in a different mood are pots of baby marigolds lined up in a copper fish poacher. A round table's garden might be a nosegay of spicy garden pinks growing in a soft blue stoneware crock, or a basket of pansies—planted in the liner if it has one, or in a moss-concealed pot. Many times the plants can stay right in the containers they come in. All you have to do is arrange these in baskets or cache-pots, with or without a layer of moss or pebbles to mask the containers. Most of these plants will bloom a week or so if they spend at least part of their indoor life in a sunny window. Some last longer than others, but eventually they all begin to show signs of pining for the out-of-doors. If you have no place to plant them yourself, it is usually easy to find a friend who does.

When you have a garden to pick from it is still an attractive idea to pot up small plants and bring them into the house for a time. And it is one solution to that universal summer-garden dilemma: Should the flowers be left to decorate the garden or cut to decorate the house? This conflict arises even when the gardener and the arranger are one and the same person. Ronaldo's solution will appeal to the gardener:

Green-and-white-striped grass, yellow-button tansy flowers, and rich green ferny wormwood, an armful of each gathered in a big copper coal bucket. The generosity of this aromatic welcome-at-the-door is a turning to advantage of a necessary piece of garden discipline: Handsome as they are, all three plants are vigorous growers that will soon swamp a garden if not severely cut back from time to time—a few stems picked now and then for bouquets are not always enough to keep them under control. Massing the cuttings in separate clumps instead of mixing them emphasizes the individual textures and creates a design that changes as you move around it—an easy, effective technique that can be applied to many different combinations of leaves and flowers.

"You don't have to devastate the garden to make bouquets. You just take one or two flowers here and there. And take them at the point when they are best to look at—mature flowers in full beauty. One more day in the garden and they would be gone. For one or two days, maybe even more, in a vase they will be a joy." A persuasive case for decorating with single flowers or small informal mixed bouquets—and even a good-sized one will not leave gaps in the garden if the flowers that make it up are in themselves large. Then, too, there are times when even the most garden-proud gardener encourages cutting. Some flowers thrive on it, and will continue to produce blossoms only if they are not allowed to set seed—cornflowers, marigolds, nasturtiums, pansies, pinks, and flowering tobacco are a few examples.

But somehow in summer the temptation to indulge in glorious masses of bloom is almost irresistible, and there are rooms which almost demand them. A sheaf of blue and violet delphiniums may be magnificent next to the fireplace, but the dozen or so stalks that it takes do make a difference in the look of the garden. The time-honored solution here is a cutting garden, if you have space for it, where you can grow in quantity and cut fearlessly the flowers you want in quantity. A cutting bed also lets you have flowers for the house that may not fit into your garden design for any of several reasons—perhaps they spread too quickly, grow too high, or have a tendency to sprawl. Or their colors may simply be wrong. One friend, who only likes to see blue and white flowers from her living room window, sets aside one row in the vegetable garden for a rainbow mixture to cut for the dining table.

The vegetable garden itself, without a single flower planted in it, overflows with materials for summer arrangements. A cutting basket of freshly picked and washed-in-the-garden vegetables can be handsome enough to go on the table just as it is. Vegetables take equally well to spontaneous-seeming still lifes or precisely planned designs: A basket of round red tomatoes, with one spray of leaves and blossoms—a healthy plant

A handful of nasturtiums loosely gathered in a yellow cream pitcher. Nasturtiums are delightful flowers for the house; they bring the sunshine right in with them and curl effortlessly into lively, pleasing patterns.

A wild garden makes a cool and keeping decoration for a terrace table. Ferns, grasses, meadow rue, violets, water plantain, trailing saxifrage, mosses, lichens, even a pair of mushrooms, each lifted roots and all from the woods, are planted as they grow, in artless profusion, in a rustic wooden basket. The only cutting needed: a few ornamental sprays of blackberry in every stage of ripeness. When they are brought to eye level you can really see and enjoy all the delicate forms and textures and colors of green that are so easily passed over in nature.

can spare it—carefully placed; a flat wicker tray heaped with glossy purple and matte-white eggplants, little radish nosegays tucked among them; one white cauliflower tightly wreathed in velvety blue-green curly kale.

"If vegetables are beautiful enough to eat," Ronaldo points out, "they are beautiful enough to decorate with. What is the difference between a cabbage and a blooming rose? There isn't any, and in fact they look lovely together. When I mix flowers with vegetables, I think of them as spice for the vegetables. You season vegetables when you cook them—instead of taste-spice, the flowers are eye-spice."

The objection is sometimes raised that the smell of certain vegetables, particularly members of the cabbage family, makes them unsuitable for decorations in spite of their beautiful forms and colors. This is almost entirely a matter of freshness. For example, you really have to bury your nose in a just-cut cabbage—from your own garden or a farmers' market—to pick up the scent, it is so faint. And that cabbage will stay almost scentless for several days if properly treated: given a good soak before it is arranged, kept out of direct sunlight, and given an occasional misting. A cabbage that has traveled several hundred miles, then lingered a week at the grocery is another matter. However, its unpleasantly strong odor is usually matched by an unattractive appearance, which makes it doubly unsuitable for decoration.

The question of scent brings up a category of plants that are grown for theirs—the herbs—and that have in addition wonderfully ornamental foliage to use with flowers, yet are not often considered. Among the culinary herbs lemon balm, all the mints, rosemary, silvery sage, parsley, feathery dill and fennel, basil—especially the purply-bronze variety called Dark Opal—and chive blossoms can be as valuable in arrangements as they are in the kitchen. Any one of them is a becoming addition to a mixed bouquet. And any one of them can be the foundation of an arrangement combined with a compatible flower—or flowers: curling red-tinged stems of peppermint with single red dwarf dahlias, purple basil with pink phlox,

A tiny touch of color—four pink verbena clusters, two pale, two bright, in an antique inkwell—for a terrace table as here, or a breakfast tray, a bookshelf, a china cabinet. When you pinch back early buds and blossoms to encourage a plant to fuller, firmer growth, do not consign them instantly to the compost heap. Their short stems are just right for miniature containers.

parsley with candytuft. The scented geraniums—rose, lemon, nutmeg—enhance almost any flower; lavender contributes both blossoms and leaves. Another group of herbs is traditionally classified as medicinal, but we grow them for their aromatic and decorative qualities, not their healing ones. Rue's pungent leaves with their distinctive blue cast have a delicate form that brings to mind maidenhair fern. The artemisias—wormwood, southernwood, stelleriana, and Silver Mound—offer astringent scents and fringy foliage, silver gray or acid green depending on the variety. The silvery-leafed ones are particularly beautiful with pink roses. Also gray or green, santolina's fine, crisp foliage is usually clipped in the garden into compact mounds and neat borders. The longer clippings, saved and bunched in vases, can be sheared with scissors into neat and charming little topiary balls and cones to assemble in a formal parterre for the center of the dining room table.

Herbs and aromatics are easy to grow. They flourish happily in pots as long as they have a sunny situation. They can even be grown indoors, but—excepting rose geraniums which seem to thrive anywhere—they need fresh air for really luxuriant growth. Yet from a four-by-six-foot city rooftop pot garden I can cut from more than a dozen different kinds all summer for cooking and for flower arrangements and still have a surplus to dry for potpourri. You need not grow your own ingredients to make potpourri—a winter pleasure discussed in that chapter—but doing so is an additional incentive, if one is needed, for raising these very rewarding plants.

With all the variety there is in it, the garden is far from being the sum of the summer's abundance.

When you really look at the shapes and colors of growing things you find wonderful material everywhere—in woods and fields and swamps, along the roadside.

It is easy to recognize the decorative potential of some common meadow and roadside flowers—Queen Anne's lace, butterfly weed,

A basket of zinnias, packed head to head to intensify
their already brilliant colors, gives a snap of life to a
mantelpiece array of blue-and-white china. There is a
freshness about a basket of summer flowers like zinnias
or marigolds or daisies that never fails to appeal, yet it is
so simple to arrange that it scarcely seems to call for
discussion. You can mass your flowers for maximum
color or space them to show off their forms and rhythms
of growth; use just one kind or color or half a dozen
different ones.

Tiny pompom zinnias gathered in a caned basket, cheerful companions for a flower-form plate
and a Chinese porcelain duck. The arrangement
was designed to make the most of their natural
sprightly movement, but because the zinnias'
own leaves decay rapidly in contact with water,
the stems were stripped of all but the pair
nearest the blossoms. The basket was filled with
a low, loose cushion of galax leaves, and then the
flowers were placed above, between, and even
under some of the leaves.

milkweed, black-eyed susan, coreopsis. But it takes an attentive eye to realize that small and humble flowers—purple vetch, blue wild geranium, yellow butter-and-eggs, white chickweed, and meadowsweet, to name only a few—can also be extremely ornamental on their own small scale when removed from surroundings that overwhelm them. We plant and pick striped and banded grasses for their decorative qualities, but rarely make use of the equally decorative plumy seed heads of common meadow grass or timothy's little green cattails. Once you forget the labels—and some of our weeds are simply energetic escapees from early gardens—you find you have an inexhaustible supply of forms and colors to play with.

There is only one important restraint on taking advantage of the wealth of wildlings. Anyone who loves flowers will cut cleanly and sparingly, leaving each plant enough foliage and flowers to reproduce itself. But some plants should not be cut at all, even when they appear to be plentiful, either because they are irreparably hurt by picking, or because they are really so rare as to be in danger of extinction. Each state has a list of protected flowers, available at the local public library, garden club, or state conservation department. And if you find some of the endangered flowers truly hard to resist and have suitable conditions for growing them, there are wildflower nurseries that can supply seeds or plants. Then, if they take, you have them to cut confidently and legally on your own property.

Summer's very riches carry a kind of irony with them. When you are surrounded with leaves and flowers, when you see green every time you look out the window, you may feel less need for green and growing things inside the house, less inclination to decorate your rooms with flowers. Yet this is the season of greatest opportunity—materials are more varied and less expensive than in any other—opportunity to make the most of. Summer is the time to experiment with new techniques and perfect them, to try your hand at complex and elaborate compositions, to make adventurous combinations and see if they please you, freely to indulge your imagination.

Three small bouquets where you would least expect them, on a bathroom counter, but one of the joys of summer's abundance is indulging in flowers for private viewing. The variations on a theme of blue and white: a topiary sphere of clipped gray santolina spangled with blue platycodon stars and raffia bows in a Japanese ginger jar; a handful of blue pansies in a tiny blue-and-white vase; and a puff of white phlox in a delftware jug.

A fragrant little posy as Victorian as the trumpet-shaped glass vial that holds it. One florist's flower, a white freesia, has crept in among the pink garden roses, pink-banded zinnias, and white phlox, but its role could easily be played by any one of a number of home-grown blossoms. Sweet pea, browallia, flowering tobacco, and stephanotis are some possibilities.

Single flowers multiplied to make a summer meadow of the table center. Flowers from the garden—bell-like white platycodon, feathery veronica both blue and white, chive blossoms, and bright pink everlasting pea branches—are mixed with flowers from the field— Queen Anne's lace, purple vetch, milkweed, and golden coreopsis. The arrangement seems random, but it is given rhythm and coherence by the coreopsis echoing the yellow Quimper plates, and the repeated circles of the galax leaves in every vase. With different china, the color of the dominating flower might be different; otherwise, you can combine at will summer's innumerable flowers and weeds. In fact, any season offers a sufficient selection for this kind of centerpiece.

Bright blue cornflowers scattered through a lacy green-and-white tangle of baby's breath, Queen Anne's lace, and penstemon. In this lively, light-handed design each stem, set in water-saturated foam in the basket's liner, is allowed space for its natural movement.

Starry red, orange, and apricot ixora blossoms massed like the nosegays in a flower-seller's basket, only here it is nature that makes the nosegay. A ruffle of galax at the basket's rim supplements the flower's own glossy pointed leaves. Ixora is a shrub related to coffee and native to Malaysia. It flourishes—and may grow up to fifteen feet—in Hawaii and the Caribbean islands. This is an easy, attractive way to arrange short stems of any flower that blooms in rounded clusters—hydrangea, daphne, azalea, rhododendron, viburnum, allium, or phlox, for example.

Fanned like a peacock's tail, a luxurious summer harvest of violet, white, and pink delphinium, larkspur, and snapdragon. The container is an ordinary plastic pail given a quick slipcover of raffia-tied tatami.

Topiary in detail: sprigs of santolina are packed as tightly as possible in the vase and sheared into shape with scissors. The flowers are a day's conceit, the topiary will last almost indefinitely — without water it will dry in the vase. In drying, it will shrink somewhat, however, for which allowance should be made in the original shaping.

A Portuguese pewter swan dressed in borrowed plumage —a haze of Queen Anne's lace. A fantasy ornament for the edge of a garden pond, as it is photographed. More conventionally, it would make a ravishing decoration for a formal dining room or for a buffet table set with crisp white linen and gleaming silver and crystal. The wing-like sweep of the flowers gives a touch of wit to the arrangement but takes careful placement, and something to hold the stems in position. Here crumpled chicken wire is used, packed tightly into the container— a better choice than foam for such a large mass of blossoms.

106

A trio of fresh-from-the-garden cabbages spiced with clusters of fluffy pink rambler roses tucked in them. The flat tray that holds them is completely concealed by the leaves. A quick composition to amuse the eye. Full-blown roses, well conditioned, will last a day or an evening out of water given an occasional misting. Then they can be reconditioned and rearranged, mounded perhaps in the liner of a flat basket or bunched in little nosegays with frills of lacy rose geranium or silvery artemisia leaves.

One cabbage like a great green rose, a cloud of starry ▶ white phlox in an antique Chinese basket. Fresh and beautiful combinations come naturally when you develop the habit of looking at each growing thing for its intrinsic decorative qualities without concern for its conventional context—weed, vegetable, fruit, flower.

108

A flock of white blossoms—Queen Anne's lace, veronica, platycodon, everlasting pea—nestle among the ruffled leaves of a single rosette of ruby lettuce, sun-burnished to glowing mahogany. A rich but lighthearted ornament for dark polished wood. The shallow white container half hidden by the leaves holds enough water to keep lettuce and flowers crisp for a day, perhaps more if the lettuce has been thoroughly soaked and drained and the room is not too warm. A little misting helps, but refrigeration does not. The abrupt change from cool to warm tends to make both lettuce and flowers wilt.

A fountain of green cinnamon ferns lightly flecked with scarlet monarda and foamy pink astilbe in a carved wood basket. The trompe-l'oeil basket is heavy enough to support their arching fronds, a real one would need weighting with stones or shot. Hardy ferns have a strong claim for a place in the flower arranger's garden: they make the most cooling of midsummer bouquets, with or without flowers.

A pair of tabletop fantasies for an outdoor buffet, either of which could stand alone. Tufts of Queen Anne's lace spring from galax rosettes set in a patchwork pavement of strawberries, raspberries, cherries, and blueberries on a carpet of moss. The necessary underpinnings: plastic to line the Portuguese fish-vendor's basket, damp foam to hold up fruit and flowers. A woven straw tray holds a pyramid of cabbages fringed with ruby lettuce, flanked by bunches of carrots, beets, and red and white radishes, punctuated with a single spire of white hollyhock. The flask that holds the hollyhock is invisible among the cabbage leaves.

A basket of broad green leaves with a random gathering of roses—red, pink, white, and creamy yellow—peeking out from beneath them makes an eye-catching doorstop. Ronaldo often likes to arrange flowers this way, "hidden between leaves so you need to look for them, like strawberries. You lift a leaf and find a surprise underneath." Here the leaves are skunk cabbage, a wild inhabitant of shady streams and swamps. The cut leaves will last for two or three days, but only if they are completely submerged in cool water for several hours or overnight before you arrange them. An equally handsome garden-grown substitute would be caladium, green or variegated, which will last even longer if given the same treatment.

A swatch of meadow brought indoors: a basket brimming with Queen Anne's lace and bright orange butterfly weed. The latter, equally beautiful in a vase or in the garden, and as its name implies a great attractor of butterflies, has achieved the respectability of the perennial catalogues. You will find it there under its Latin name, *Asclepias tuberosa.* It is very cooperative—easy to grow, easy to arrange, and adaptable to an enormous variety of decorative inspirations.

Flowers and grasses arranged naturally just as they grow: fluffy orange butterfly weed loosely mounded in a basket and punctuated with spikes of timothy; stiff pennons of bulrush set straight in a sturdy brown jug. Two or several all-of-a-kind bouquets grouped with an eye to contrasts of shape and texture make a fresh and striking alternative to the mixed bouquet. The scale can be grand or miniature. The colors can be all the same—a tall basket of pink larkspur with a shorter basket of pink cornflowers and another of pink phlox, for example—or different—yellow daisies replacing the cornflowers, white rather than pink phlox. The mood, charming or splendid, romantic or graphic, depends on the individual personalities of the materials—which are given full play in this kind of presentation.

5. Fantasies and Celebrations

Fantasy for a small and private celebration: a magic carpet of fresh green galax leaves starred with gardenias, narcissus, and lace flowers thrown over the table transports dinner to a forest glade for the evening. To create the illusion, galax leaves are sewn from the center in an overlapping spiral to cover a round tablecloth completely. The thread should be dark green and it only takes a stitch or two around the mid-rib to anchor a leaf. If the cloth is expendable, the leaves can be glued to it, which makes the work go faster. The cloth can be made a day ahead, and the flowers added at the very last minute, tucked among the leaves on the table surface, pinned to the skirt. If this seems too time-consuming a decoration for a very small party, consider how enchanting such a cloth would be for a bridal-shower buffet or for the table that displays the wedding cake.

Just one flower in the house brings a touch of festivity to everyday, but everyday is not all of living, and for the happy high points—holidays, anniversaries, weddings, birthdays, or just parties—you want flowers to do more, to communicate the spirit of the occasion. Decorating for a celebration is more than a matter of more flowers, although it usually means that, too. If generosity is the heart of festivity, for Ronaldo its language is fantasy.

"You can't separate parties from fantasy. When you create a party you are creating fantasy. You are creating an environment, whether it lasts two hours or twelve hours, to pick everybody up in a mood to enjoy, to have fun. Let your imagination wander. You can give the feeling that you're in China, or at the court of Louis XVI, or on a summer picnic in midwinter. Or maybe you cannot tell exactly where and what it is—that's the point of fantasy."

Ronaldo's fantasy designs are not always evocative of the long ago and far away. Sometimes they spring from a feeling about some aspect of nature or about the source of the celebration; a party for dancers, for example, suggests the idea of balance as a theme. The forms that yours take will depend on your own sense of the occasion's mood and upon the visions that fuel your imagination. There are certain practical aspects to creating an illusion, however, and various strategies that are helpful in insuring that your decorative ideas create their intended effect. They are useful when you are decorating your own house for a party, but even more important to keep in mind when you are faced with the problem of decorating a large public space—a hotel ballroom, an auditorium, a church, a club. Whatever the occasion, the first consideration is the nature of the space.

"Guide yourself with the first instinct you have when you come into a room," Ronaldo advises. "Don't fight the room, but fit the things you add into it. Coordinate your lines with the room's lines. If you give me an Art Deco room and ask me to make it Victorian, I can't do it with flowers. Unless I can drape the entire room, I can't make it in any way Victorian. For the same reason, I cannot create in a very formal room the feeling of a relaxed, understated Japanese dinner."

Seen on these pages, flowers of the four seasons in formal bouquets decorate a living room turned ballroom for a birthday gala. Suggested by the French eighteenth-century style of the room's paneling, this "fantasy of a court entertainment" is in fact a twentieth-century luxury. Even royal greenhouses of the period would have found it difficult to assemble all the seasons at the end of September.

A last-minute ornament, a chandelier's flowery pendant was improvised on the spot when Ronaldo noted that very tall guests might bump into the low-hanging fixture. He looped a handful of lacy smilax vine over the chandelier, caught them together with raffia-tied hydrangea clusters, and tucked in a few cosmos and freesia to make the most decorative of warning signs.

In front of the French doors at one end of the room, big bouquets are raised to dancers' eye level on delicate iron pedestals which Ronaldo brought in for the occasion and which he finds endlessly useful for giving flowers the height they need in a space filled with people. Cascades of silvery green eucalyptus leaves with their matching buds and blossoms and lighter green hydrangeas echo the pale almond of the paneling. A slender spire of bare branches symbolizes winter; a scattering of bright flowers samples the rest of the seasons—lilies, gerbera, alstroemeria, stock, sunflowers, white euphorbia, goldenrod, and one crimson tulip, all but the tip of a petal hidden from the camera. Ronaldo first built the basic shape with the bare branches and eucalyptus in the chicken-wire-packed terra-cotta containers, then added the single tall stalk of lilies and the fluffy hydrangeas, and finally the colorful accents.

On the mantelpiece a fantasy flower garden—purple iris, sunflowers, red and yellow tulips, pink and white ranunculus, white freesia, and double crimson cosmos all blooming out of season—is flanked by a pair of porcelain birds, the permanent inhabitants, and tall slim bouquets of bare branches, lilies, cosmos, sunflowers, gerbera, alstroemeria, and green hydrangeas in clear glass cylinders. The flowers are planted in a long narrow foam-filled container completely concealed by a mossy manteltop lawn.

◀ A terra-cotta cherub, one of the room's regular ornaments, given a basket lantern and a load of leaves and flowers bigger than he is, becomes a lighthearted, light-bearing party decoration. The bouquet of eucalyptus, hydrangeas, lilies, gerbera, cosmos, alstroemeria, and tulips is arranged in a moss-covered container slung from the neck with barely visible wire and propped with a bamboo pole to stabilize its weight. The lantern, a vigil light in a Japanese bamboo basket, has its handle wedged in the split end of another bamboo pole which is then wrapped and tied with raffia. (For further information on the creation of this piece, see Chapter 10.)

117

◀ Three tabletop flower beds—a fluffy mosaic of blossoms flanked by taller, narrower, more open plantings—decorate the dining table for the same birthday party.

A tuft of orange alstroemeria is circled by a colorful mixture of pink-spotted rubrum lilies, purple anemones, blue lace flowers, pink roses, yellow freesia, and white Queen Anne's lace. The flowers and their ruffled border of galax leaves almost completely conceal the round moss-wrapped container.

Slender sprays of red montbretia, a trio of apricot tulips, two budded stems of pink nerine, a low-growing stalk of white lilies, clusters of pink roses, blue lace flowers, yellow and white freesias, a sprinkling of Queen Anne's lace, rosettes of galax, and trails of ivy seem to spring from a narrow strip of mossy lawn. In fact, the moss conceals a narrow foam-filled container and the flowers in this fanciful garden are all cut.

Red nerines replace pink ones and the roses are yellow. Otherwise this little flower bed is a twin to the one at the opposite end of the table.

If the room has a distinctive character it will be easy to focus your choices. Unfortunately, a great many public rooms are so bland, when they are not actively unattractive, as to have no discernible character—the average school auditorium, for example. They may give more freedom to your imagination, but at the same time they make it more difficult to carry out your imaginings. With an unlimited budget, of course, anything is possible. This is almost never the case and the time, money, and materials that a complete masking takes are usually out of the question. The answer is not to try to conceal the awkward or inappropriate features in a room but to direct attention away from them.

When a space is too large or too tall to decorate completely, you can suggest an environment simply with the placement of your decorations. Height is important. Unless decorations are at or above eye level they are not likely to be seen at all in a room full of people. The specific height of eye level depends on whether guests will be seated or standing when they are in the room, but decorations placed at any point you choose above it will catch and hold the eye within the illusion you wish to create. Ronaldo acknowledges that finding containers to hold flowers high is a problem, and he often has to invent some sort of pedestal to raise up his bouquets. Other possibilities to consider are lined baskets or moss-covered containers attached to the walls, garlands of leaves and flowers, or hanging baskets. Sometimes Ronaldo uses tall trees to solve the problem. For one midwinter reception in an armory, he set all the tables in circles around graceful palms and ficuses—two very easy-to-rent trees. "It takes more tables to do this because you lose one place at each table, but you have a lovely feeling of dining outdoors under the trees."

You can also direct attention where you want it to go by concentrating your decorative efforts in one or two areas. Even when the room is a beautiful one, a few large designs, lavishly executed and strategically placed, will create with the same quantity of materials a far greater impression than dozens of skimpy scatterings. At times the occasion will tell you where to

Mossy tiers rippled like the brims of picture hats drip violets in a whimsical variation on a Victorian epergne, and more violets and graceful grape hyacinths are tucked in the frill of galax leaves that circle its base—irresistible romance for a Valentine supper or a bridesmaids' lunch. The flowers will only last the length of the party; violets may bring good luck, but they are notoriously short-lived. The epergne is made of sturdier stuff and could enchant a whole series of parties garlanded with any suitably romantic flowers. The central support is a half-inch dowel set in plaster of Paris in a round metal container. The tiers are squares of chicken wire with a cross cut in the center, slipped on the dowel, folded into shape, and wired securely in place. A shallow circle of water-saturated foam goes on top of the plaster, more bits of foam in the center of the tiers, and then the whole is finished off with a coat of moss.

Architectural in its simplicity, this very twentieth-century fantasy was created to decorate a cocktail reception for a ballet company. A cylindrical glass vase is solidly packed with long-stemmed tightly budded mauve-and-green-banded allium, all but four of them bound with raffia in a straight stiff column rimmed with galax leaves. Tied in pairs and weighted with silvery dried flower heads of sea holly, the remaining stems bend in springy balancing curves. The bamboo and fabric structure that frames the arrangement was made by Brazilian artist Paulo Nobre.

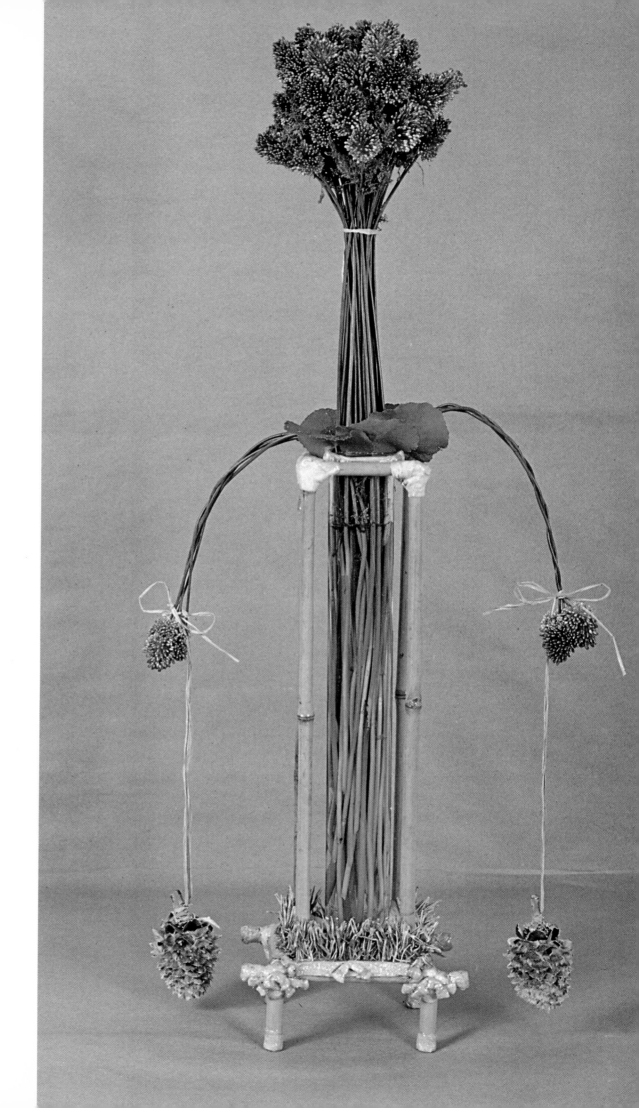

Another variation on the theme of balance, another decoration for the ballet reception, demonstrates that wit and surprise can be as festive as charm and romance. Rubrum lilies in test tubes tied with raffia to each end balance a green-stem crossbar that is lashed, also with raffia, to four stems of foxtail lily. Tufts of moss separate the plumy flower heads, a bow-tied collar of moss tucked into the neck of the vase wedges the stems upright.

A thatch of straw shades a straw-wrapped container filled with blue lace flowers and green-and-white striped grass, a playful touch that for Ronaldo creates a fantasy. "What fantasy? For me it suggests Marie Antoinette playing milkmaid. Others see it as a small oriental gazebo or a South Sea island hut. That's the joy of fantasy—it can be whatever speaks to your imagination." The roof, a handful of straw tied with raffia and fanned in a circle, is supported by a simple framework of sticks lashed together with raffia and set in the foam that fills the container.

put your emphasis. At a wedding, for example, all eyes will be on the ceremony and the decorations logically gather themselves around the spot where it takes place. In most cases the location depends on the room. Sometimes there is a natural focus, an architectural element like a fireplace or an alcove, or, in a long narrow room, the two ends.

Many of Ronaldo's big party designs, especially when they include many tables to be covered, depend as much on color as they do on flowers or leaves to make over a space. Sometimes table flowers and tablecloths are all the decoration he gives a room, and it can be extremely effective. One reception comes to mind. With all the tables skirted to the floor in peppermint pink and centered with topiary balls of red, white, and pink roses and Queen Anne's lace, you never noticed that the room itself was both low-ceilinged and decidedly undistinguished. As long as it is the color you need, the fabric for table coverings can be of the cheapest kind—plain cotton dress goods or sheets, for example. Theatrical supply houses are a good source for inexpensive burlaps, gauzes, and lamés when you want texture or glitter. If it is to count, however, fabric must be used generously, and you often get better results by spending less of your party budget on flowers and more on tablecloths.

Or on candles—glowing and flickering, they can almost decorate a party by themselves. Lighting is a great creator and intensifier of mood. Concentrating the illumination where you concentrate the decorations, subduing it elsewhere in the room if the situation allows you to control it, is one of the easiest ways to maintain the illusion you have created.

The opportunities to create elaborate fantasies for large parties and once-in-a-lifetime celebrations are not as frequent in most of our lives as they are in that of a professional designer in flowers, but once in a while they do occur. Professional strategies are as applicable to the dinner and cocktail parties that are our more usual festivities, and these, if on a smaller scale, are as much occasions for fantasy.

Spiky yellow-orange allium heads tied in tight bundles sway on their tall and wiry stems over a clear glass pool of water filled with shiny black pebbles and sprigs of moss: a fantasy water garden that might have materialized from some science fiction planet.

◄ Two rows of precisely graduated tuberoses are tied to a frame of bamboo cane in what Ronaldo calls "the geometry of the garden. This is a plantation owner's view of things growing." But even in this well-ordered garden there are weeds: a few freesia buds poking up through the moss. The narrow tatami-wrapped tin is filled with moss-covered foam.

A single giant sunflower soars over a clump of yellow star thistles to make a spectacular arrangement nearly four feet tall. "This is not fantasy, it's nature," says Ronaldo. "Sunflowers always stand alone and all the other flowers grow beneath them." To hide the thistle stems, two leaf-patterned brown batik napkins are gathered into petal points that echo the shape of the sunflower leaves, tucked into the neck of the vase, and tied in place with raffia.

Frothy white baby's breath spirals around a conical topiary tree, one of a pair that, set on the chancel steps, frames the altar for a green-and-white wedding. This tree was manufactured of branches, but privet is easily clipped and tied in symmetrical shapes; a living bush could be substituted, its root ball wrapped in green cotton just as the container here is. For the altar bouquets, more green-and-gold privet branches are mixed with white lilies, carnations, and Shasta daisies.

Pendants of baby's breath and smilax topped with a single gardenia and crisscrossed with white ribbon streamers mark each pew. A twist of wire, concealed by the bow, ties the baby's breath and smilax; its ends are taped to the pew. The gardenia, also taped to the pew, is added at the last minute to minimize the possibility of anyone brushing against it and bruising and browning its petals.

Decorations for the wedding reception ▶ are also green and white, their design inspired by the setting, a restaurant famous for its Art Deco style. On each table, a glass globe circled with galax-wrapped vigil lights is filled with a fragrant mixture of stock, freesia, madonna and calla lilies. Tall silver columns capped with palm-fringed silver crescents ring the dance floor. Tucked into the top of each are a vigil light and a single spray of white orchids in a glass flask. The columns are sturdy cardboard tubes—carpet rollers would work very well—covered in mirror-bright Mylar and set in heavily weighted green-wrapped cylindrical containers. A circular shelf is fastened inside, a couple of inches from the top, to hold the vase and candle. The flat fan-like capitals—two sheets of silvered cardboard cut to shape and stapled together with the palm fronds sandwiched between them—are wedged into a slot in the shelf.

Romantic in itself, the horse-drawn carriage that takes the bride and groom from the church to the wedding reception is still more romantically garlanded with ribbon-wrapped streamers of asparagus fern and bouquets of pink mountain laurel. The finishing touch: a basket of daisies with a split of champagne and two glasses tucked among the flowers.

Decorations designed for a summer wed- ▶
ding in a country church make the most of
the handsome materials to be found in
summer fields and gardens. Cut by the
armload from a meadow full, three-foot
stalks of yucca—a flower that demands use
on a grand scale—are combined with bul-
rushes, wild grape vines, white phlox, and
pink rambler roses to make a monumental
bouquet, one of a pair to flank the altar.
The green smilax that festoons the pew is a
florist's standby and not home-grown, but
the roses and feathery grasses twined into
it are.

To decorate the buffet, palm leaves and white gladioli—a
classic Art Deco combination—are fanned in a green Art Deco
vase improvised for the occasion. It is one of the tall galvanized
metal containers that florists use for conditioning flowers,
smoothly wrapped in dark green cotton with pleated fans of the
same fabric basted on at the rim and base.

131

A Victorian doll's wooden wagon wreathed in roses and smilax
carries, on a cushion of rose blossoms, two gold wedding rings
tied with a raffia bow—a fresh and appealing decoration for the
bride's table.

Great swags of wild grape vines and fluffy pink roses turn a garden gazebo into a retreat for the bride and groom to share a private toast. It would also be a very romantic setting for the wedding cake. All the wedding party carries pink rambler roses—the bride a few loose sprays lightly bound with tendrils of ivy, the bridesmaids tight nosegays swirled with galax leaves, and the youngest of all a basket full. "For the bride I like the flowers to be very loose and fragile. Brides have a kind of trembling in the body that's very special, that only happens that one time, and the flowers should move with the body. Bridesmaids' bouquets I make very compact, almost Victorian, so they don't compete."

Lavender tablecloths and moss baskets wreathed in softly colored flowers dress all the tables in a large country club dining room for a wedding supper. In each basket the flower mixture varies; here we have rubrum lilies, pink roses, blue lace flowers, yellow freesia, violet anemones and allium, apricot alstroemeria, and white Queen Anne's lace.

For a midwinter dinner dance, a midwinter fantasy: bare and bushy branches tied in a tall panache express the mystery of flowering in winter. Rubrum lilies bound on with moss and wire are sprinkled among the twigs; white tulips and lemon leaves cascade from the spot where the branches divide, their moss-covered container attached with invisible lashings of fine green wire.

◄ Here the trees are twiggy branches radiating from a moss ball raised high on a branch trunk—their basic construction is demonstrated in Chapter 10. The branches bloom by artifice, not miracle: lilies, freesia, and a scattering of galax leaves are bound to them with wisps of damp moss secured by a twist of wire. Only the tables were decorated for the party, which was held in an art museum, and they gave a room full of splendid paintings all the extra festivity it needed.

137

6. The Moods of Autumn

Three white freesia, a daisy, and a pink rose in a green pear-shaped vase. Here nature supplies the container instead of inspiring the potter: the pear is real. And seasonal, unlike the seasonless flowers. For container purposes you need a pear of the firm fall-and-winter kind, a green Anjou or Comice or a russet Beurre Bosc. Unripe and cored to hold a tube of water for the flowers, it will last at least as long as they do, but it cannot be recycled for eating.

What makes a flower arrangement autumnal is almost more a matter of mood than it is of materials. And autumn's moods are as various as its weather—John Keats's "Season of mists and mellow fruitfulness" one day, a crystal clear sky and the tonic snap of frost another. Heat waves may follow hurricanes in the three-month tug of war between summer and winter that winter will finally win with the first sharp freeze. Until then autumn fields and gardens are very nearly as generously endowed with colors and shapes and textures to arrange for the house as are summer ones. Many of summer's flowers go on blooming right up to the frost, or can be made to do so by succession plantings—gladioli, for example. Others, like summer itself, make return appearances, brief but brilliant. Given a good year and the right varieties, you can have roses and delphinium to cut in early November. Autumn contributes flowers of its own to the whole spectrum, so you can if you wish plant to continue your summer color scheme right through the fall.

Certain kinds and combinations of colors seem especially autumnal. For most of us, the picture of autumn color that forms instantly in the mind's eye is one of rich and glowing reds and yellows and oranges, tawny rusts and golds, burnished browns and mahoganies—the hues of autumn leaves. The leaves themselves are the final blaze that ends the season; their coloring is a strand that runs all through it. Along with the lingering summer bloomers—achilleas, calendulas, dahlias, marigolds, and zinnias—come sunflowers large, small, single, double, annual, perennial, and in every shade of red, orange, and yellow. Add to these rudbeckias, gaillardias, gloriosa daisies, cockscomb and plumy celosia, salpiglossis, montbretias, cardinal flowers, late-blooming sedums, deep-red Michaelmas daisies, and all the gold and bronzy chrysanthemums and you still have not listed all the flowers in autumn's richest color range, not to mention its equally ornamental crop of berries and fruits, seeds and pods. Only the colored leaves with which the season is so prodigal are of doubtful value for decorating the house.

"I like colored leaves, but out-of-doors. That kind of arrangement nature does better than anyone else—great drifts of color that are to be seen from a distance." Ronaldo's feelings are confirmed by experience: frost-colored leaves are usually disappointing in bouquets. They never seem as brilliant indoors, and their lasting qualities are extremely problematical. Most seem to curl and shrivel very quickly in the warm air of a house. The only ones I have had success with are those whose color is intrinsic and not frost-given—bronzy-purple copper beech leaves, for example, or the fine-cut red or green-gold foliage of Japanese maples—and those only when cut before they are well into the natural process of detaching themselves from their branches.

Welcome as warmth is late in the season, in early autumn the most appealing colors lie in another part of the spectrum. Green arrangements in general and green flowers in particular are a marvelously refreshing change from summer's rainbow brilliance, and September has plenty of days hot enough to need refreshment. There are green flowers to be had in all seasons, in fact, but the early autumn ones have an especially interesting variety of forms to work with. Green zinnias, flowering tobacco, sweet-scented mignonette, tasseled love-lies-bleeding, various spurges, lady's mantle, snakeroot, and gladioli in both standard and butterfly forms are among the better-known of these. Also, several varieties of hydrangea, *H. paniculata grandiflora* in particular, turn green late in the season. Green is uncommon enough as a flower color, however, so that it can take real detective work to find some seeds and plants. I still have not located a source for a green dahlia, a green spider chrysanthemum, and two green clematises, *C. rehderiana* and *C. orientalis,* although I have seen all of them alive or in photographs. Green-flower bouquets make lovely decorations for pale rooms or wood-paneled ones—too-colorful surroundings tend to overpower their subtle and for the most part delicate tones. But if you have the right environment for them, green-flower collecting can become addictive.

Fortunately, you need not take up this rather specialized pursuit to enjoy

Glowing purple heather tied into a topiary tree dries without changing color. The arrangement, however, must be made fresh; dehydrated stems are too brittle to bend into shape. To make it, tall spikes of heather—the tallest in the center and as many as the container will hold—are set in a block of dry florist's foam cut to fit the Imari bowl, gathered together about two-thirds of the way up, and tied tightly with wire. The top-knot is then bound with wire into a smooth finial. For autumn, the heather tree is finished off with a raffia bow and some silvery curls of aromatic oakmoss. Come Christmas, a red velvet bow and a lavish sprinkling of little marzipan strawberries and peaches and oranges renew it in the spirit of the season.

the refreshment of green bouquets. Foliage arrangements can be just as interesting, and leaves come in so many shapes and shades of green that you can put together combinations to complement a room of any color. Still vivid after many years, so successful was the effect, is the memory of a brilliant Chinese yellow hall decorated with a rather formal composition of curly kale, white-ribbed chard, and green-and-white variegated hosta and ivy.

It takes no special planting to have plenty of material for foliage arrangements. Only frost puts an end to most of the summer greens—ferns, grasses, reeds, and herbs as well as leaves. There are at least as many kinds of vegetables, both leafy and compactly shaped. Add green fruit—grapes, plums, apples, pears, quinces—and you have a considerable repertory of forms and shades to design with.

In fact, you do not need a garden at all. Farm stands, farmers' markets, and even city vegetable and fruit stores have seasonal produce fresh enough to be decorative, although for best results it needs good conditioning. True, a stroll through the garden will give a greater variety of foliage than a visit to the flower shop, but most florists have some selection of evergreens like laurel, lemon, magnolia, rhododendron, and eucalyptus. The richest range of beautiful foliage for the city dweller is to be found in house plants— begonias, coleus, marantas, peperomias, cissus, and all the ivies plain and variegated, to suggest a few possibilities. Cutting a few leaves for a bouquet will not spoil the looks of the plants. It may even improve them, and besides, many of the leaves will root in water, giving you new plants to pot up once you decide to dismantle your arrangement.

Green leaves make the substance of many of Ronaldo's autumn compositions, with the flowers used just as accents. Aromatic gray-green eucalyptus is a special favorite and with it he combines flowers in still another autumn color vein: a soft range of pinks, yellows, creams, whites, misty mauves and blues, occasionally touched with clear red. His flowers are greenhouse-grown gerberas, tuberoses, Shasta daisies, roses, lilies, lilylike members of

Reds marshalled in close harmony for an autumn centerpiece—slim sprays of crimson montbretia in rosy-red porcelain bud vases, tight nosegays of red-and-gold tulips in moss-filled cinnabar-red lacquer bowls. That tulips can scarcely be called an autumn flower does not seem to matter, so strongly does the coloring suggest the season, but for consistency they might easily be replaced by ruby-red Michaelmas daisies or dahlias, or rusty pompon chrysanthemums. The votive lights wrapped in galax leaves and tied with raffia are almost a trademark with Ronaldo. He feels strongly that "candles on the table should either be very low or else very high. It's tiring when you have to look straight at the flames all through a meal."

142

the amaryllis family—nerines, lycoris, amaryllis belladonna, vallota—and his pet flower-for-all-seasons, freesia. With a garden you can have an even greater variety of forms and textures in the same color feeling. Cosmos, cleome, petunias, phlox, gladioli and large-flowered hybrid clematises carry over from summer. Careful study of the catalogues will turn up late-blooming lilies and most of them list the hardy pink amaryllis, *Lycoris squamigera*. Autumn's own offerings include rose-of-Sharon, delicate Japanese anemones, autumn crocuses, crocus-like yellow sternbergia, Arctic daisies, Michaelmas daisies in misty blues, pinks, and lavenders as well as white, plus buff, pale yellow, pink, and mauve chrysanthemums in different forms and sizes.

Long lasting, easy to grow and ship, chrysanthemums are an ideal flower for commercial growing. Anyone who has to depend on flower shops for flowers and is without access to the more varied wares of the big-city ones might be forgiven for thinking that chrysanthemums are all there is to autumn. Since the discovery that they will flower at any season, given a certain number of hours of darkness, they have become a year-round as well as an autumn staple. Perhaps because of their very ubiquity—or the stiffness of their stems—Ronaldo rarely uses them. You will not find any in this chapter's arrangements, but in many cases they can easily be substituted for the flowers he has used.

In giving a sense of season, the shaping and presentation of materials are as important as color, Ronaldo feels, and more important than whether or not the materials are of the season.

"Autumn for me is nostalgic. It's when you think of leaves falling and revealing the lines of the branches. I like arrangements to be more sparse, more open and linear. I like to show stems or raise up the flowers to show the ground."

Ronaldo's sparse arrangements may be casual bouquets—a half-dozen or so long-stemmed flowers and a few sprays of leaves or berried branches—but more often they are highly stylized. He will plant a row of tuberoses or

Wild inhabitants of autumn fields groomed into a little garden for the table: a bush of pokeweed branches laden with red-stemmed berries in every stage of ripeness, a knot of purple joe-pye weed, a patch of green moss lawn. Their handkerchief-size plot of land is a foam-filled baking tin with a raffia-tied tatami wrapper.

Late summer weeds and flowers by the armload fanned in a tatami-covered pail, a bouquet suited for drying as arranged. Among the ingredients—which include Queen Anne's lace, dill, cattails, wild mint, spurge, purple allium, white larkspur, and yellow thistles—only the orangy plumes of eremurus or foxtail lily are unfit for drying. You can still dry the arrangement, however. If all soft leaves are removed from the part of the stems that will be immersed in water, you can enjoy the bouquet fresh for a few days, then remove the eremurus for another arrangement and let the water evaporate. The rest of the material will dry naturally.

146

An exuberant mass of santolina temporarily decorated with yellow hawkweed. The foliage is already several days into the natural drying process that will finish with its silvery color and aromatic scent intact but its mass slightly reduced. Because it will stay where it is as long as it is wanted, it has only a square fence of logs bound together with raffia for a container. The whole composition is the serendipitous result of a garden clean-up: the foliage clipped from a santolina border in need of tidying, the logs cut from a storm-felled tree, and the hawkweed extirpated roots and all from the lawn.

scarlet vallota in a narrow moss lawn and give them a bamboo fence for support; or bundle flowers together and tie them with raffia into self-supporting, long-stemmed formal nosegays; or set a moss-covered topiary ball on a tall branch and stud it with flowers and leaves. Since each flower is in its own water pick and can be removed and replaced as it fades, these mock-topiaries can be used again and again, and given a different look with different colors and shapes of flowers.

Autumn provides an abundance of plant materials with the gift of persistence, and Ronaldo takes advantage of these to make a variety of long-lasting decorations with replaceable parts: a stalk of lilies rising caduceus-like from a bed of statice, a basket of bittersweet and lilies, a mound of santolina starred with yellow daisies. The statice, the bittersweet, and the santolina will all dry as arranged and last through the winter or until you tire of them; the lilies and daisies can be replaced because they each have a separate source for water. In some designs each flower stem is in a water pick; in others, a bud vase is concealed in the foam that holds the dried materials. The principle is a simple one and endlessly adaptable. The basic arrangement can be casual or stylized, composed of any kind of dried or evergreen material, and given a fresh look with each change in flowers. It is also an easy, attractive way to make a big decorative effect with a very few fresh flowers, welcome in winter when they are greenhouse-grown and expensive.

Even without the addition of fresh flowers, dried bouquets can be extremely handsome decorations, and Ronaldo's technique for making them requires no complicated procedures.

"Flowers dried chemically are hard to handle and difficult to arrange. They look stiff and not natural. So do most of the ones that have been hung upside down to dry, even if they are dried naturally. The easiest, and I think the most successful way is simply to pick materials that you know dry well, arrange them when they're still fresh and flexible, and then leave them alone and let them dry by themselves. Put the arrangement somewhere, though,

Cattails held in soldierly uprightness by tufts of moss and galax leaves screen a collection of porcelain vegetables and garden-decorated china—a spare but evocative arrangement for early autumn.

Two white lilies, two yellow ones, three ▶ stems of scarlet nerines, two creamy white gerberas, and a trio of eucalyptus branches informally but carefully arranged in one of the spare and open compositions that for Ronaldo express the spirit of the season.

A month later the same bouquet has dried to a soft and subtle blend of pinks and creams—the hydrangeas —and beiges—the goldenrod. The mood has changed and so to a small degree has the size of the arrangement. Most flowers shrink in drying—hydrangeas and goldenrod less than many—which is why it usually pays to be generous with your materials in composing bouquets for drying.

A basket heaped with richly colored bronze-and-green hydrangeas punctuated with plumy goldenrod. The flowers are fresh and freshly arranged but not in water; the bouquet is designed for drying. The stems are stripped of their leaves, placed in the container, and left to dry in place. This is perhaps the simplest technique for creating dried-flower decorations, and the one Ronaldo considers the most successful. Graceful compositions come so much more easily when flower stems are green and flexible.

where there is not going to be a lot of traffic brushing against it while it's drying. Hydrangeas are one of the nicest flowers to dry this way, and goldenrod, and all the autumn grasses."

These are bouquets in the most sober and soft-spoken of autumn's moods, the coloring of post-frost fields—creams, beiges, ambers, silvery greens and grays, russets, tans, and browns. Subtle as the colors are, the shapes and textures of all the flowers, leaves, grasses, and seed heads that lend themselves to drying are so varied that they can be composed to create almost any style of arrangement to suit a room of any kind and color. Some examples that suggest the range: a classic black basalt urn compactly and symmetrically mounded with yellow and white achillea—the Coronation Gold variety will keep its color dried, the white will turn creamy. A jet of cattails shooting high from the center of a low basket filled with a tangle of curling ferns—ferns will twist themselves into marvelous convolutions if cut green in various stages, tightly furled to fully open, and dried as arranged. A big romantic bouquet in every shade of brown and beige that mixes a dozen different materials. Or one that is all silvery, whose ingredients might include dusty miller, pampas grass, pearly everlasting, several artemisias, blue salvia farinacea, garden sage, thistles, and sea holly. Or the easiest kind and one of the most adaptable—a simple informal basket arranged as you would one of field flowers, using as few or as many kinds of material as you like.

The season for making dried bouquets is a long one—any time from midsummer on through November. Finding the materials is mainly a matter of looking and experimenting, there are so many things that can be dried. If you are not sure about something, try it out in a small arrangement. Ronaldo's arrange-first-dry-later method makes it easier to achieve graceful bouquets, but it does depend, for large arrangements at least, on being fairly certain about the behavior of your materials. You will find that many leaves and flowers shrink in drying. You can overstuff to allow for this, or you can turn it to advantage. New material, fresh or dried, can always be added to a dried arrangement and many times the best ones are built in stages. Whether or not you use some kind of support material—chicken wire, florist's foam, sand—for your arrangement depends as it does with fresh flowers on the character of the arrangement and the container. One common complaint about dried bouquets is the tendency of some materials to shatter and shed. Most authorities recommend as a preventive measure a light spraying of clear plastic; but one friend who is famous for her dried weed bouquets prefers to use unscented hair spray.

Naturally dried bouquets can be more colorful than those we have discussed: this most wintry of autumn's moods is as checkered as the rest. Many of the season's bright berries dry well—as a rule of pinch for choosing them, the firmer the berry, the better it keeps its color and shape—and among the everlasting flowers quite a few varieties are colorfast: yellow and red celosia; pink, lavender, and blue statice; red, terra cotta, gold, and buff strawflowers; purple, red, and yellow globe amaranth; pink, purple, and lavender heather.

Dried bouquets, however, are not the only gifts that autumn makes to winter. It is as much a season for planting as for preserving, and the bulbs that you pot for forcing in October will give winter the pleasure of spring flowers.

One perfect artichoke impaled on a candleholder offers its
vegetable architecture to embellish a dinner tray. The stem,
hollowed out to fit over the candlecup, is tightly bound with
raffia for support and decorative finish. It would be needed only
for the latter purpose had its candleholder base been fitted with a
candlespike instead of a cup.

◀ Fruit and vegetables in a new and different decorative role. The
green pear bears a pink rose, one acorn squash holds a white
anemone and the other a leafy spray of euphorbia fulgens. There
is a little deception involved—the flowers do not depend for
their water supply on their apparent containers. Ronaldo simply cuts a hole just big enough to insert a tube—a kitchen
coring knife is the perfect tool—in any firm-fleshed fruit or
vegetable that suits the color scheme he has in mind.

Miniature heather topiaries, each one different, are casually grouped on a
low black lacquer table, two growing from tiny silver sacks, the third from
a galax-covered votive glass. In Ronaldo's hands heather seems to turn
naturally into fanciful shapes. To create these openwork forms, he first
constructs the shape in wire, then wraps it in flower stems, a technique he
demonstrates in Chapter 10. They are a little complicated to make but
reward the effort by lasting as long as you want to keep them, and by
lending their whimsical charm, as engaging on the dining table as it is in
the living room, to any place you want to put them.

A fountain of aromatic silvery-gray eucalyptus leaves
is the foundation for an opulent autumn bouquet that
includes green-bronze hydrangeas and long-stemmed
ornamental pineapples, all of them very nearly everlasting, spiced with more transitory autumn
flowers—tuberoses, scarlet nerines, pink
alstroemeria, creamy gerberas, and soft yellow lilies.
The basic arrangement will last for weeks. As the
more evanescent accents fade they can be replaced,
and with each renewal of flowers comes a chance to
vary the mood and the colors. For example, you
might substitute soft pink, mauve, and buff spider
chrysanthemums, pale blue Michaelmas daisies, hot
pink nerines, and plumes of purple heather. Or, for
a very different feeling, russet or gold chrysanthemums, yellow and red gaillardia, apricot alstroemeria, and bright and dark red gladioli. Water-
absorbent foam, mounded above the rim of the
container—a tall tin-lined cylindrical basket—and
covered with a dome of chicken wire, allows the
foliage and flowers in this bouquet to radiate in all
directions. To maintain the arrangement's keeping
qualities, it is important that the foam be kept continually moist. Once it dries it does not readily
reabsorb water. When long-lasting greens or flowers
are arranged in water instead of foam, a piece or two
of charcoal—but not the treated kind sold for
barbecues—in the bottom of the container will help
keep the water fresh and free of bacteria.

Starred with zinnias and loosely garlanded with tendrils of silver-lace vine, a moss-covered topiary ball makes a high-rising centerpiece. The stem, a half-inch wooden dowel, is set in a foam-packed flowerpot and tied with a flowing raffia bow. Tabletop topiaries like this are extremely effective party ornaments and extremely adaptable ones. You can decorate the same basic form to suit any season or color scheme and to be as fanciful or as architectural as you wish.

7. What Do You Do With a Dozen Carnations?

The adaptable glass globe, quadrupled and stacked, turns some red tulips into an arresting decoration.

Or roses? Or chrysanthemums? Perhaps you bought them—that bundle of color was so appealing in the shop that you could not resist it. More likely they were a present and one you appreciated—who can ever have too many flowers? But when you come to arrange them you find it a problem to make an interesting decoration with a dozen or even two dozen flowers all of a kind and color, particularly when, like these three all-season florist's favorites, they have long, stiff stems and are very often leafless or have leaves awkwardly placed from a designer's point of view. However grateful one is for the skill and investment that give us flowers whenever we want them, it is frustrating that some of the sturdiest and most readily available kinds are also some of the most unbending—chrysanthemums and gladiolus—and that commercial growing seems to require breeding out the natural grace of others in favor of the specimen blossom. Not all florist's flowers, of course, are such problems. Tulips, freesia, most lilies, and miniature carnations with their branched and budded stems fall naturally into graceful bouquets. It is the stiff-stemmed ones that offer a real challenge to the arranger.

What *do* you do with a dozen carnations? You make the most of their virtues: those beautiful blossoms. And cut the stems without hesitation to whatever length will show off the flowers most effectively. Long stems have no particular decorative value in themselves, they simply give you flexibility. You can adjust the height of the flowers to suit a wide variety of containers. If you visualize your bouquet in a setting that requires height, you can have it. If a low mound of color seems more appropriate, all it takes is cutting. And with cutting your flowers will often last longer—a secondary bonus.

When Ronaldo arranges carnations he takes his cue from the blaze of color that gives them such allure in the flower shop and bunches them into tight nosegays, borrowing a presentation favored by European flower-vendors. Sometimes he tucks in filaments of moss to give each flower its individual outline, sometimes he treats the whole fluffy mass as a single giant flower. He may make a virtue of the long stems and bind them into a

Gladiolus leaves and budded stems shoot up in a green aurora from a cluster of pale peach blossoms. Commercially grown gladioli are cut in such tight bud that usually only a few blossoms on a stem are open when you buy them. Cutting the stems short to mass the bloom at the rim of the container turns half a dozen stalks of a flower that is often considered nearly impossible to arrange into a spirited decoration.

tall column, or cut the stems short and heap the nosegays in low bowls or baskets. These are techniques he uses as often for roses as for carnations, and sometimes even for mixed bouquets. It is also an attractive way to compose many of the chrysanthemums, the large fluffy kinds as well as the button, pompon, and daisy-flowered varieties.

Less stylized but equally colorful are bouquets made by placing each flower individually in the vase but with all the blossoms touching each other, literally head to head. This is Ronaldo's preferred technique when the flowers are fragile ones like daffodils or ranunculus, or when he feels a setting calls for a single splash of color. The shape of the arrangement—a tall pyramid, a soft sphere, or a low crescent mound—depends on the form and rhythm of the flower and on the shape of the container. When you have just a dozen flowers to work with, neither container nor arrangement can be very large, but when you are fortunate enough to be able to count your flowers by the dozen, the results can be extremely impressive. Flowers by the dozen are not always such an extravagance as they sound. Even in big city shops certain flowers in season are cheap enough—often less than a dollar a dozen—to use with a lavish hand. And there are occasions that justify extravagance: fifty golden roses or a hundred bright yellow carnations make one of the most spectacular presents imaginable for a golden wedding anniversary.

And a very much appreciated one, providing you send it ahead. Unless your florist knows the household and the kind of arrangement the recipient likes, it is usually nicer to send loose flowers. But however pleasant an occupation, composing an arrangement does take attention and a certain amount of time. When a guest arrives flowers in hand for a party, time and attention to give them are conspicuously lacking. Still, it happens to all of us. The custom seems to be widespread in this country, although in most of the world it is considered ill-mannered, and flowers are sent either early in the day of the party so they can be arranged at leisure, or the following day

Plump flower spikes of shell-pink gladiolus massed in a pyramid of long-necked glass vases. To give the blossoms center stage the stems are stripped of their leaves and most of the green-budded tips pinched off. This is not such a waste of potential flowers as it seems; the topmost buds of greenhouse-grown gladioli rarely open. And, if the tips are long enough, they can be tucked in to accent the arrangement, as is the case in this bouquet.

In a graceful and inventive demonstration ▶ that gladioli can be arranged for charm as well as drama, the flowers not only fill a moss basket but form its handle as well. Crumpled chicken wire in the shallow moss-covered container provides the underpinning for the two tall stems bent in a gentle arch and tied together near their tips with a raffia bow; for the paired fans of leaves and buds; and for the carpet of single blossoms and short-stemmed blossom clusters.

Yellow daffodils, closely spaced to make a single splash of sunny color, are placed one by one in the container, a gourd packed with water-soaked foam. The tallest stems determine the height of the arrangement; the others are cut to fill in the design. This cheerful panache takes four dozen flowers, but daffodils, although short-seasoned and short-lived when cut, are very inexpensive in season, often well under a dollar a dozen. You can mass them generously without feeling spendthrift.

Giant football chrysanthemums, each flower treated as a nose- ▶ gay in itself and set on its own crystal globe, are lined up precisely on a tortoise-colored bamboo tray as they might be lined up on a dining table.

Nine pink carnations in a frill of galax leaves fill a square bamboo basket, or seem to. In fact, their tightly bound stems are set in a bud vase inside it. Little wisps of pale green moss threaded through the bouquet let each flower show its shape without diminishing the color impact of the whole. The flower seller's nosegay is a European tradition that adapts itself to a setting of any style—here it happily joins an Indonesian palm-leaf fan on a Japanese lacquer table.

Red rosettes on a mossy mound—oversize carnations, each made up of six blossoms—decorate a round buffet table. It takes two dozen flowers to make this centerpiece, but in a smaller bowl for a smaller table it could be duplicated with three-blossom nosegays. The container is a shallow bowl completely covered with glued-on galax leaves—the technique is demonstrated in Chapter 10—and filled with a shallow dome of chicken wire to support the moss and flowers.

One dozen white carnations bound up into one giant carnation—a fresh and eye-catching presentation that turns the long, stiff stems as well as the fluffy flowers of this year-round favorite to decorative advantage. It could not be easier to make. A bow-tied band of raffia holds the blossoms together; the long narrow neck of the crystal carafe, collared at the rim with galax leaves, clasps the stems into a reeded column. You start by gathering and tying the flowers into a smooth dome, then cut the stems off evenly and insert them in the vase, which must have a narrow neck—decanters make perfect containers—but can be cylindrical or rectangular as well as flask-shaped. Many different long-stemmed flowers take to this bundling technique—familiar ones like chrysanthemums, roses, snapdragons, and plumy celosia, and less-known ones like some of the alliums, foxtail lilies, liatris. The shapes of the arrangements will vary with the architecture of the individual flower. When stems are thickly leaved, the foliage can be included in the design. Foliage can be added, like the galax ruffle, or the design can be just a simple graphic line of stem and blossom.

as a thank you. Even when you are the only guest for a lunch or dinner, flowers given on the spot are a distraction that dims the hostess's enjoyment of the gift. Ronaldo suggests: "If you feel you must bring flowers, bring a single blossom in a bud vase. It is all arranged, all your hostess has to do is set it down."

When you are confronted with the problem you have two choices. One is simply to put the flowers in a bucket of water out of the way—in the kitchen or even in the bath tub—and arrange them after the party is over. The other is to provide yourself with the kind of container that will arrange almost any flower presentably, drop the bouquet into it to enjoy for the occasion, and refine the arrangement later. A glass globe, generously sized, is Ronaldo's candidate for the all-purpose container, but almost any simple, wide-mouthed shape seven or eight inches tall will accommodate all but the very tallest or smallest of flowers attractively. So will a collection of bud vases, which you can either group or distribute around the house.

Bud vases offer an easy solution to arranging a dozen flowers even when you need not do it in a rush. Or you may want to take out one or two of the most perfect ones to present singly before you compose the rest.

When florist's flowers have attractive leaves of their own, these can be used to help shape the design. If they are leafless you can add compatible foliage from another plant. Unfortunately the leaves that usually accompany gift flowers are either banal—asparagus fern—or so stiff as to be useless in an arrangement—huckleberry—and are best considered simply as packing materials for the flowers. If you go to the flower shop yourself, however, you can almost always find interesting foliage. It takes no more than Ronaldo's favorite moss and galax leaves to give a nosegay a green frame for its color—a good argument for keeping a supply of both in the refrigerator. Ronaldo creates some of his most charming arrangements with leaves as the primary element, perhaps filling a container with a carpet of ruffly galax or lacy leather-leaf fern and scattering the flowers throughout in separate jewel-like accents. Several of these arrangements, using a mixture

169

Bunched in a dense mosaic, rose-pink roses, hot-pink nerines, yellow daffodils, red-and-gold-striped tulips, purple tulips, and violet anemones glow with stained-glass brilliance. Even when a florist's bouquet gives you more than one kind and color of flower to design with, extending the range of possible presentations, you may still find the nosegay makes the most striking decoration. And if you cannot bring yourself to chop off all the stems of a freshly delivered box of flowers, this is a wonderful way to recycle the survivors after dismantling a larger bouquet that has begun to fade.

A nosegay of nosegays in close harmony mixes roses in two shades of pink, carnations in a third, and red-purple tulips. Massing the flowers in little bundles emphasizes the individual texture and color of each variety. Any one-color bouquet is more vibrant when the flowers that compose it are actually in several different hues of the same color, even if they are all the same kind. A medley of carnations in red-orange, scarlet, crimson, magenta, and deep rose-pink, for example, makes a really blazing red bouquet. Foliage is not needed for contrast, but the pair of rose leaves peeping out at the lower edge gives an appealing touch of informality to the very symmetrical arrangement.

An antique scale fitted with holders for a dozen ▶ bud vases can arrange a dozen of anything, at least any but large and heavy blossoms. The character of the arrangement depends on the shape of the flower and the length of its stem. With the long-stemmed freesia in the photograph the arrangement is open and airy; round and short-stemmed flowers would make little carpets of color.

A half dozen bright-yellow tulips, each in its
own glass flask, are casually grouped on an
oriental export porcelain platter. A collection
of bud vases is a great aid when you have to fix
flowers in a hurry. The most time-consuming
part of this arrangement is filling the containers
with water.

◀ Four white porcelain vases packed in a picnic
basket play host to half a dozen white anemones.
Moss holds the flowers upright in the vases;
chopsticks lashed in a grid to the rim hold the
vases steady when the basket is carried.

An open but quite symmetrical bouquet of
twelve daffodils makes its decorative point not
with a burst of color but with the shapes and
rhythms of the individual leaves and flowers.

Nosegays of pink rosebuds laced with moss and ▶
ruffled with galax leaves are heaped with a prodigal hand to make a festive centerpiece. Each
little bouquet is itself a charming ornament,
and an attractive present for each guest to take
home when lunch is over. When nosegays are
packed this tight they support each other—no
wire is needed in the galax-covered bowl—but
those at the top should have slightly longer
stems so they can reach down to the water.

of flowers, appear in other chapters, but they can easily be adapted to flowers of one kind and color. Many of Ronaldo's garden flower bouquets in fact will suggest ideas for arranging the florist's wares.

In decorating with any kind of flower, its individual characteristics are more important than whether it is grown in a garden or a greenhouse. The essential point is to consider the flower itself—its shape, its color, its texture, the rhythm of its growth—and create your design from whichever aspect or combination of aspects strikes you as the most decorative or most suitable for the setting you have in mind. Some flowers take extra thought and attention, but then they reward you with a little extra thrill of triumph when you succeed in finding the right composition for them.

Six tulips in compact instant arrangement. Tulips are so graceful that they compose themselves effortlessly in almost any container, but this round glass globe, set for the moment on a porcelain sweetmeat dish, is one in which almost any bouquet of flowers will fall into an attractive pattern.

8. The Resources of Winter

In a hospitable and portable arrangement, gourds filled with nuts and dried prunes share a bamboo-slat tray with a vase of pink roses. Meant for eating as well as looking—the fruits and nuts are easily replaced—it has moved right onto the sofa to join some other basket-borne refreshments.

Whether you look on them as winter luxuries or winter necessities, plants and flowers to decorate the house are not gifts of the season but pleasures acquired in defiance of it. Only in Hawaii and those narrow bands on the hardiness map of the United States marked zones 9 and 10 is winter truly a growing season. Through most of the country nature offers for cutting some bare branches, a few berries, and the hardy evergreens, all of them useful materials for arranging but comprising a rather limited repertory.

One way to increase the variety of your resources is to move the garden indoors for a supply of materials and as a decoration in itself. You do not need a greenhouse to have a winter garden, although having one will give you a wider range of planting possibilities. So many kinds of plants will grow in the rooms you live in that your garden can be as lavish as you wish.

A winter garden of greens is the easiest to grow. There are foliage plants for every combination of heat, light, and humidity that you happen to have or can contrive. And they come in enough different shades and shapes and textures of green to allow a wide variety of decorative effects, formal or jungly.

A winter flower garden used to be more difficult to create, but since the introduction of light bulbs specifically designed to encourage growth and bloom, it is no longer necessary to have a south window, or indeed any window at all. Plant lighting has also expanded the range of plants that can be brought to bloom in winter in ordinary household conditions. Some of the most surprising things will flourish. For one example, flowering tobacco, a summer annual, will grow from seed and blossom in a north window all through February and March with the aid of a plant light. So great is the winter appeal of flowering plants that more and more varieties are being specially bred for more spectacular blossoms and a longer indoor blossoming season.

Flowering plants are independent creatures, however, and will not always bloom just when we want them to. Even indoor gardeners some of the time, like most of us most of the time, have to look for their flowers to

179

those larger winter gardens, the commercial greenhouses and, thanks to air freight, the tropical regions of this world. The flower shops' greenhouse-grown flowers offer a selection of the seasons to design with—spring freesia, narcissus, daffodils, tulips; summer stock, delphinium, daisies, cornflowers, lilies; autumn chrysanthemums. Flowers from the tropics, Ronaldo feels, belong more specifically to winter. "In my winter arrangements you see a lot of orchids, a lot of tropical flowers—anthurium, heliconia, euphorbia. Warm, sunny tropical flowers inside the house trying to balance the cold outside, that's my Brazilian warmness mentality."

It is unfortunate that just when we most want the warmth and color that fresh flowers give, they are the most expensive to buy. Tropical flowers at least mitigate some of their cost with their keeping qualities. Orchids will last a couple of weeks cut, anthurium even longer given conditions they like. What they do not like are drafts and too hot, too dry rooms. Care in placement will solve the first problem, a humidifier is probably the best answer to the second, since hot dry air is as unhealthy for people as it is for flowers.

Making a few flowers count for a lot of decoration is another strategy, and one at which Ronaldo is adept. Large arrangements may take advantage of interesting containers that do not require quantities of blossoms, or they may be composed of leaves or dried materials with a few fresh flowers for accent. When impact is not needed he turns most often to single flowers, placed to give wit or charm to a collection of objects. As refreshment for the eye, a single flower is perhaps the most affordable of winter's pleasures.

Like flowers the flower-given pleasure of fragrance—as much an ornament to the house as color and form if appealing to another sense—seems to be more appreciated when it is least easily available. In the seasons when it comes naturally in leaves, flowers, and in the complex and subtle perfume that is fresh air, we tend to take it for granted. But in winter, when the windows are closed and the flowers are scentless, it becomes something to cherish. To cherish year round, it must be added, in big cities where the

Supple pussy willow stems, each looped and tied with raffia, then all bound together in a whimsical calligraphic bouquet, spring from a galax-collared glass carafe.

180

Pussy willow calligraphy illuminated with
flowers—pale yellow lilies, a daffodil in bud,
and two fragrant white freesia—is flanked by
softly glowing candles, vigil lights in candle-
sticks created by artist Paolo Nobre.

Branches of forced forsythia twined together ▶
and tied with raffia arch over a basket of
daisies—an inspiration as lighthearted as the
dancing Chinese porcelain deity beside it. The
flowering handle is not really attached to the
pandanus basket; the branches, like the flowers,
are embedded in the water-saturated foam that
fills the basket's liner.

184

Refreshing the whole room with a sweet scent of spring, a basket of green ferns dappled with white roses and fragrant paperwhite narcissus lights up a gray winter day.

scents of nature's air are often overpowered by chemical effluvia. It seems a strong statement to say that winter flowers are scentless, but very few of the tropical flowers have any aroma, and most greenhouse-grown flowers have had it bred out of them—roses and carnations are dramatic examples. The exceptions are spring flowers. Forced hyacinths, narcissus, and freesia keep their fragrance when cut as well as they do growing in pots, one of the many reasons why they are so appealing in winter. Orange and lemon trees, gardenias, and jasmine also make excellent winter-blooming fragrant potplants. It takes no more than one pot of any of them to scent a room.

For more enduring fragrance you can turn to the flowers that keep their aromas when dried—lavender, roses, jasmine, orange blossoms. These, along with dried herbs, citrus peels, spices, and aromatic woods and resins are the raw materials for all the scented mixtures that go by the name of potpourri. Potpourri-blending is a very ancient branch of the art of perfumery and the easiest to practice. The ingredients are not difficult to find and need not be expensive, and the pleasure of creating a potpourri of your own is almost as great as the pleasure of having it in the house.

Scented mixtures can be as simple or complex, delicate or pervasive as you want to make them. Perhaps the easiest way to illustrate the techniques of potpourri-making is to take one recipe through a series of possible variations.

A blend of dried herbs, the basic recipe consists of two cups rose geranium; one cup each lemon verbena, lavender, woodruff; one-half cup each rosemary and thyme. Mix them all together thoroughly in a bowl, crushing them gently in your hands. Put the mixture in an air-tight container like a two-quart Mason jar and leave it for about a month to let the odors blend, giving it an occasional shaking. However the ingredients vary, this is the method for blending any potpourri. This mixture gives a very fresh and delicate fragrance. You will not really be aware that there is a bowl of it in the room unless you dip your hand in and run it through your fingers. But many times you want only a hint of fragrance, and delicate

185

◀ Rosy-cheeked apples are neatly piled in a pewter basket with the aid of bits of moss tucked in to check their natural propensity for rolling. Effective and inexpensive winter decorations, pyramids of shapely, colorful fruit—oranges, lemons, limes, grapefruit, persimmons, or pomegranates, as well as apples—are easily maintained when you simply use bits of natural greenery to keep them in line. Fresh herbs or sprigs of evergreen substituted for the moss would add scent as well as stability.

Like a swarm of tiny yellow butterflies, oncidium orchids bring two weeks of tropical sun to a winter room. A tuft of moss and trio of galax leaves in the neck of each glass bud vase shore up the slender wiry stems; otherwise these delicate and intricate little flowers are presented as simply as possible.

scents like this one are particularly nice packed in little pillows to tuck into your bed or into bureau drawers, linen closets, or suitcases. It is the easiest and least expensive kind of potpourri, but the most evanescent, lasting little more than a couple of months.

A longer-lived version is created by the addition of fixatives. These are aromatic substances—resins like benzoin or frankincense, roots like vetiver or orris, seeds like tonka or ambrette, animal extracts like musk or ambergris—that absorb and slow the evaporation of more fleeting scents. They both prolong the life of a potpourri and add depth to its fragrance. Two crushed tonka beans and a heaping tablespoon of powdered or crushed benzoin added to the basic recipe will make the scent richer and longer-lasting without changing it. It will still be a delicate one—potpourris made entirely of dry materials never really project their fragrance.

A truly pervasive potpourri requires in addition to fixatives a combination of essential oils, minute traces of which give the dry ingredients their natural fragrance. About three and a half pounds of lavender flowers, for example, are needed to make one ounce of essential oil of lavender, and about 250 pounds of petals to make one ounce of essential oil or attar of roses. Essential oils are so concentrated that they do not even smell like the herbs and flowers from which they are extracted when you sniff them in the bottle. They should be used with a *very* light hand. Three drops each of the oils of rose geranium, lemon verbena, lavender, and one each of thyme and rosemary are all that is needed to transform the recipe into a potpourri capable of scenting a large room or a small apartment. Mixtures that contain essential oils are more expensive to make and it takes longer to blend them—at least six weeks in an airtight container—but they will often last for years. Whenever they show signs of fading you can renew them with fresh applications of the same mixture of oils in the same small quantities.

The strength and longevity of a potpourri are matters of technique, the fragrance is one of personal creativity. Once you have decided how strong and how lasting a scent you want, you can start on the fascinating business

Potpourri in a green jade bowl draws an audience of agate animals—an amusing tribute to the magnetism of its fragrance.

◄ Scarlet gerberas, simply arranged with three of their own leaves in a pale celadon porcelain vase, join with two large and shapely crystal jars to create a tabletop still life. Handsome as they are, gerbera leaves are not often available at flower shops. Green ti leaves are acceptable and more available substitutes. Or you might try large leaves from house plants like dieffenbachia, aglaonema, or spathiphyllum.

A branch-handled moss basket filled with sprays of white cymbidium orchids and decoratively patterned maranta leaves makes an exotic and long-lasting winter arrangement. Although the composition is an informal one, the strong shapes of the leaves and flowers are felicitous companions for Frederick Wehmer's dramatic stylized portrait of a crocus, seen through the doorway.

191

of composing that fragrance. Just by varying the proportions of the different materials in the sample recipe you can create a dozen different scents. There is almost no limit to the additions you can make. Add cloves and orange peel and you have a spicier scent, add rose petals instead and you have a sweeter one, to give only two examples. Any recipe, and there are books full of them, is simply a starting point for the exercise of your olfactory imagination.

The technique described is that for making dry potpourri, which you can make at any time of year. If you have a garden, you can grow and dry your ingredients, but you can buy them as well as the fixatives and oils from local herb and spice shops, drugstores, or from any one of several mail order suppliers. In the sample recipe only rose geranium is sometimes hard to find commercially, but it grows as vigorously indoors as out, and in a few months clippings from one pot will give you all you need. The grocery store can supply many materials—peels from oranges, lemons, and limes, a number of herbs, and all the spices.

There are two other kinds of potpourris that should be mentioned, although they have more specialized requirements. In moist potpourris, which many experts consider the longest-lived, the flowers and leaves are not fully dried and must be prepared and added to the mixture as they come into season. To make them you need a garden, and if you have one the technique is worth looking into as a summer pleasure.

Professionally-made potpourris like the ones Ronaldo is known for are still different. They are really perfumes—complex compounds of essential oils and extracts—sometimes with as many as thirty different elements in the blend. The dry ingredients are simply carriers and need have no scent of their own at all. These potpourris are sophisticated, long-lasting, and extremely pervasive, but, depending as they do on so many different essences, they are not practical to make in household quantities. It can cost more to assemble the raw materials, when you might have to pay thirty dollars for a quarter ounce of an oil and you need only a drop of it, than it

Flowers fresh and dried combine to make an aromatic winter decoration for a bookshelf arrangement of books and memorabilia. The basket is filled with a sweet-scented mixture of dried herbs and flowers, the bud-vase holds a fresh bouquet

of Queen Anne's lace and freesia. Tucking a single flower or a little bud vase bouquet in a bowl or basket of potpourri is one of Ronaldo's favorite ways of making potpourri as attractive to the eye as it is to the nose.

does to buy the potpourri made up. The pleasure of potpourri-making need not be inhibited by this kind of expense. You can appreciate complexity without having to emulate it.

What you can adapt from the professionals are their ideas for making potpourris look as attractive as they smell. Ronaldo often decorates his with petals or whole flowers dried chemically so that they retain all their color. Flowers dried in this way lose their scent, so they can perk up the appearance of crushed and powdered material without affecting its fragrance. Flower-drying compounds are readily available, but if you do not want to bother with the drying you can use equally scentless everlasting flowers like globe amaranth, statice, or strawflowers for a dash of color and shape. A few of the aromatic ingredients kept whole and added to the finished mixture will also give it a more varied and interesting texture. Depending on the blend you might consider some nicely shaped rose geranium leaves, two or three cinnamon sticks, sprigs of oakmoss, leafy twigs of bay or rosemary, long curls of orange peel, little pine cones.

A major contribution to the visual attractiveness of potpourri is the container in which it is placed. It makes a marvelous excuse for displaying beautiful pieces of porcelain, but almost any container in any material that suits the style of your room can be pressed into service. About the only practical consideration to keep in mind is that potpourri will need renewing less often if the container has a cover and can be kept closed at night or when you are away from home. On the other hand, potpourri in an open bowl, continuously perfuming the air, creates one of the nicest welcomes-to-the-house, the first breath of fragrance as you walk in the door.

There is a spirit of welcome as well, Ronaldo feels, in arrangements of seasonal fruit. He often composes little coffee-table still lifes with baskets of dried fruits and nuts, or else stacks oranges or tangerines or apples into precise and ornamental pyramids.

"It takes patience to make them, but you don't have to use sticks or wires that perforate the fruit to hold a pyramid together. Just pile up your fruit

An airy egg-shaped basketwork bag turns a few flowers into a dramatic coffee-table decoration. It is opened just enough to let a pair of pink lilies, another of red anemones, a white anemone, a few sprigs of white freesia, and a little knot of daisies wrapped round with galax leaves peek out from the foam-filled container concealed in its interior.

Bright red anthuriums lend month-long color to a swirl of feathery palm leaves, an arrangement as lively as the Japanese bronze carp beside it, but not quite as long-lived. Still, foliage bouquets are among the most durable of winter decorations and it takes surprisingly few flowers to light them up. Any number of different flowers, from narcissus to chrysanthemums, could replace the nine anthuriums. More perishable flowers would simply allow more frequent color changes.

◄ Delicate white orchids, their curving stems laid in a casual, graceful garland on a black lacquer table, decorate a dinner for two. However fragile they look, orchids are quite sturdy, stay crisp for hours out of water, and could easily ornament the table for a week of dinner parties. Between appearances they should stay in a cool, draft-free place, their stems in a glass of water.

hole flowers, dried chemically to keep
eir shapes and colors, are added for eye
peal to a naturally dried mixture of
ushed leaves and flowers composed for
ent. With a container as handsome as
is antique Chinese porcelain bowl, the
ented mixture could really stand on its
·n.

Typical of the sumptuous containers made
in eighteenth-century France specifically
for potpourri is this shallow covered bowl
of lapis lazuli mounted in gilt-bronze.
Potpourri keeps its fragrance longer in a
covered container and it is surprising how
quickly that fragrance will spread through
a room once the cover is removed.

The classic potpourri container for those
who prefer to keep the air of their rooms
continually perfumed is a generous bowl
like this antique oriental one. The aroma
can be revived with an occasional sprinkling of brandy or even more effectively
with a few drops of the essential oils used
in the original blending.

◄ Miniature pineapples top mounds of
galax leaves at the four corners of a
stainless-steel-topped coffee table.
The long stems of the pineapples
reach right to the bottom of the
tatami-wrapped juice cans packed
with water-absorbent foam that rises
a few inches above the rim to give the
galax leaves an underpinning. These
are a florist's fruit, meant for decoration and not for eating. They will dry
naturally in place, making the arrangements reusable throughout the
season, refurbished with fresh galax
leaves as needed.

very carefully. Tuck in little bits of moss where you need to give them
stability—the way they use tissue paper in a fruit store. Or, even better, use
bay leaves or rosemary or any kind of herb with a nice fresh smell. Use
containers that make sense though—trays or baskets, big brass buckets or
early American wooden ones. When you arrange fruit this way anyone can
pick up a piece and eat it. You can replace it easily. It's a decoration that you
use rather than just look at."

Winter hospitality calls on all the season's resources—fruit and fragrance, flowers and plants, evergreens and branches—in the weeks of
festivity that stretch from Thanksgiving to New Year's Day, but decorating
for the holidays is such a special opportunity for exercising the imagination
that it has a chapter of its own. In the house, if not the garden, the holidays
seem to bring winter as well as the year to an end. With the New Year come
the pussy willows and forsythia, the forced flowering bulbs and branches
that transform the last months of winter into the first season of spring.

One touch of life, a single overhanging anemone, turns a collection of miniature objects—a silvered bridge, a file of china ducks, a bright red bus—into a playful tabletop landscape.

◀ Flowering touches for a kitchen corner—a yellow lily in a glass of tulips, a solo daisy in a crystal flask, and, tied by its neck to a nail in the wall, a daisy-packed bud vase.

◄ Candles in the window—votive lights alternate with starry bursts of white narcissus the length of a bedroom sill. Half-hidden behind the pillows, eucalyptus leaves in a silver swan add an astringent note to the sweet scent of the narcissus.

Gold-edged crimson Rothschild lilies shoot stars of bright color through a clump of heliconia. Heliconia with its broadsword leaves and stiff stems of boat-shaped flower bracts—these are pinky beige, but some varieties have brilliant red bracts and yellow flowers—is a long-lasting winter present from the tropics to flower arrangers.

201

9. To Finish the Year With a Flourish

Tiny moss deer walk warily through a forest of bright red tulips on a candlelit Christmas table. All it takes is a coat of moss to transform inexpensive little plastic animals—toy and variety stores have all kinds of them—into fresh and charming ornaments. Look for animated shapes, paint them all over with white glue, and when it is tacky press on a thin layer of moss.

There is nothing so stimulating to the imagination as a party, and with all the festivities that crowd around its four great holidays, the end of the year is a party forty days long. It can last even longer; some enthusiastic celebrators carry on through Twelfth Night and the Chinese New Year. In the spirit of general rejoicing, all the separate symbols and traditions that we associate with Thanksgiving, Hanukkah, Christmas, and New Year's seem to merge, and in decorating for this special season there is almost no limit to where you can let your fancy take you. Your decorations can echo the color and style of your rooms if you choose. Or they can be designed to create a whole new mood, and they need not be elaborate to do so. The traditional Christmas tree, its ornaments collected over a lifetime and related not by design but by the meanings and memories they hold for the family, works its magic by its own existence, independent of its surroundings. You can find your inspiration in the traditional materials and colors of the northern Christmas—red and green, white and silver and gold—or turn to another festive tradition—the hot pinks, reds, oranges, and purples of Mexico, for example—that you find more sympathetic. Or make a break and fill your house with pink and white flowers—narcissus, tulips, amaryllis, cyclamen, azaleas. For Ronaldo, "Christmas is a time to look at things not with the eye of sophistication but with the eye of childhood. It is a time to let your mind go back, to play, to be naive and colorful."

Birds and animals make a special appeal to Ronaldo's imagination and the lively moss and boxwood menagerie that he creates for Christmas is a fantasy straight from childhood. But for all their air of spontaneity, these creatures, large and small, take some skill to make. They are fabricated of foam and chicken wire in the same way as his topiary balls and cones are, but the shapes are much more complex. Once you have mastered the technique with simple shapes, however, the challenge is really to your patience. The reward for the time spent in making one of these cheerful beasts is that it will last through the whole holiday season. If your animal's coat is moss, he can even be popped in a plastic bag and stored for another year, but by the

Christmas topiary: a napkin-wrapped basket of sheared boxwood dotted with kumquats and two tame fawns with red ribbon collars. These moss deer are fabricated of foam and chicken wire, their soft green coats bound around them with fine green wire. The standing one has shiny black button eyes, his companion sports a pair of tiny real horns.

◄ Another member of Ronaldo's moss menagerie, a curious giraffe, is dressed up for the holidays with a big pink rubrum lily.

A jolly green teddy bear offers as his holiday welcome a bamboo scoop of potpourri.

The traditional turkey, ringed with bright red apples, plays his traditional star role on a quilt-covered Thanksgiving table, but this jaunty boxwood bird is just for looking. Tied and sheared into shape, the classic topiary technique, from a bush of tightly packed boxwood branches bound firmly with wire, he has a star-of-Bethlehem beak and more of the same flower to decorate his tail. The blossoms will need replacing but the turkey will live to decorate the dinner table all through the holidays. His plumage will be glossier if his feet are kept wet and he is given frequent mistings, but even dry he will hold his shape and color.

A spectacular decoration and a topiary tour de force, this larger-than-life boxwood crane is poised so naturally that you expect him to turn his head at any minute. The technique is the same as that used to make simple ball-and-stem topiary trees, but it takes both sensitive observation and considerable skill to create the framework—a complicated structure of foam, wire, and bamboo in a plaster of Paris base. Covering the frame is relatively easy—twigs of box are poked into the wire-covered foam to clothe the body and bound with fine wire around the neck and legs. The finishing touches are a horn beak and a few dried reeds tucked into the moss-covered base to give the crane his accustomed habitat.

following Christmas his coat will have dried to a golden brown, which in the right setting can be as attractive as the original green.

Topiaries in all the simple stylized shapes of shrubs and trees turn up over and over again in Ronaldo's holiday designs, and all the forms he uses in other seasons have their holiday dress. His Christmas trees for the most part are Christmas-tree-shaped boxwood constructions, which have a lot of advantages, particularly for apartment dwellers. They are easy to size for their setting, easy to move, and last longer in indoor heat then do needled evergreens. Their ornaments may be very simple—a scattering of kumquats, lady apples, or marzipan fruit. Or whimsical—a colony of fuzzy little teddy bears. Or spectacular—masses of flowers that almost overwhelm the green.

Most of his inspirations are found in nature and executed in natural materials. Even when they seem unconventional, like trees and garlands made of hay, spring flowers for Christmas, or baskets of potpourri and spices, they have a link to tradition, as a glance at the verses of old carols will demonstrate. But when the occasion calls for it, Ronaldo does not hesitate to use any resource that will create a festive flourish, giving traditional candles, for example, all the reinforcement that modern materials like silvery mylar and gleaming lamé can provide.

What counts in holiday decorating is a feeling of festivity, not where your inspiration comes from or what materials you choose to realize it. They can be humble or precious, familiar or exotic, natural or man-made. You can follow traditions or invent them. Any decorative impulse that expresses your personal sense of celebration will suit the spirit of the season, for it springs from the joining of two festive traditions far older and more generous than the specific holidays we commemorate: the rejoicing and sharing of the harvest, and the celebration, in the year's darkest days, of the promise of light and life renewed.

The Christmas playground for a trio of teddy bears is a big bundle of boxwood cuttings stuffed into a wooden tub and sheared into symmetry. A happy flower-bearing wooden cub swings high over the tree from a branch trestle, while his furry companions wait their turn in a nest of straw. The single votive light is stabilized in a flat-bottomed straw basket.

211

◀ Candlelight and glitter give the New Year a luminous welcome. For a dance held in a planetarium, season and setting both suggested decorations with the color and sparkle of a clear winter night. To reflect the night sky overhead, Ronaldo sheathed the dance floor in silver Mylar, covered the tables in deep blue lamé—an inexpensive one from a theatrical supplier—and starred the room with candles in silver votive glasses. They shimmer in a ring around the dance floor and sparkle in glass-globe pyramids on the tables, lighting up their star-of-Bethlehem satellites. For this party the most spectacular part of the decoration came with the room, but lacking a planetarium setting one might create a similar effect by crisscrossing a ceiling with strings of pinpoint Christmas lights.

In a whimsical mixture of the artless and the artful, a calico-clad china doll smiles from a hay wreath lavishly decked with silk flowers in red and pink, lavender and apricot, and tied with ribbons of garnet velvet. Pink satin ribbons anchor the wreath against the looking glass.

◀ An everlasting tabletop topiary of plastic boxwood decorated with multicolored, frankly fake flowers is constructed around a candletree designed for votive lights. The galax leaf wrappings that conceal the holders make the candles seem to float among the flowers.

A column of red-and-white-striped candy canes makes a Christmas container for a froth of starry white narcissus blossoms. These canes are plastic look-alikes glued to a cylindrical plastic refrigerator jar and finished off with a striped and dotted red, white, and green ribbon, but they could as easily be the real thing. The container would be more fragile—candy canes are noted for their brittleness—and strips of florists' clay would be a better adhesive than glue.

A cluster of white narcissus and a simple red band decorate a pair of spruce wreaths bound together with a fringe of boxwood tucked between them. Also tucked between them and securely fixed with wire is an unseen glass flask to hold water for the flowers.

A flower-strewn boxwood garland tied with streaming bows of ▶ raffia falls in a graceful swag from a pair of tall silver candelabra to make a fresh and fragrant centerpiece for a formal table. Like most green garlands this one is made by binding leafy twigs around a length of twine with fine, flexible wire.

Little moss deer half-hidden in the foliage give a lighthearted touch to this most extravagant of Christmas trees: a boxwood cone banked with fresh flowers, all with their stems in water picks. Little baskets of potpourri and raffia garlands strung with dried rosebuds add still more fragrance to the delicate spring scents of the fresh blossoms.

◄ Miniature straw baskets of lavender blossoms, wisps of aromatic oakmoss, nosegays of mauve and pink silk flowers, and clusters of artificial fruit make softly colored decorations for an unconventional but sweet-scented hay Christmas tree decked with raffia bows and little brass and silver charms. Tiers of moss-covered chicken wire attached to a long dowel give the tree its structure.

Royal purple silk iris with golden beards—rich but un-traditional Christmas coloring—are clustered with sprays of green fabric leaves at one side of a billowy hay wreath. The wreath is simply a length of hay garlanding tied in a loop. To make it, handfuls of hay are bound at their mid-points around sturdy but soft twine with raffia.

Green velvet streamers and knots of pink silk rosebuds give this hay wreath a very eighteenth-century air. To make bows stay crisp and streamers stay as placed, florists use wired ribbons, which can be ordered from florists' supply or display materials companies if your local flower shop does not have them.

◀ A generous festoon of white pine branches and a flowing raffia bow transform a simple spruce wreath into a lavish but subtle outdoor decoration. Even though plain spruce wreaths you can buy made up are rarely as full as you would like them, they have one great advantage. Making ever-green wreaths from scratch is a messy undertaking—pitch is hard to remove from hands and clothes and wearing gloves is no aid to dexterity. It is much easier to add extra greens to ready-made ones or simply to buy two of the same size or of overlapping sizes and wire them together.

The flower-arranging supplies that Ronaldo works with are, clockwise from the florist's knife, a roll of stem-wrapping tape, a handful of flower picks, a bundle of quarter-inch wooden dowels, a brick of water-absorbent foam, a piece of half-inch bamboo, a spool of green enameled wire, a pair of wire cutters, a bowl of charcoal, a tray of live sheet moss, a folded square of chicken wire, a hank of raffia circling a plastic spray bottle, a roll of paper-wrapped green florist's adhesive clay, and three plastic water picks or vials. All are arranged on one of his favorite container-wrapping materials, a length of the woven grass called tatami or goza in Japanese, China matting by the Chinese.

10. Tools, Techniques, and Tricks of the Trade

Many of Ronaldo's arrangements are so simple that you have only to look at them to know how they are made. They require no special materials or technique and just one tool—a well-honed carbon steel paring knife (few stainless blades will take or hold a sharp enough edge to cut flower stems cleanly). Nothing more is really needed, but in flower arranging, as in all crafts, there is a great deal to be said for equipping yourself with tools and materials of professional quality and learning professional techniques. Then, when you have an inspiration, you have at your fingertips the materials and the knowledge to bring it into being. In addition to lists of basic materials for flower arranging and where to buy them, you will find in this chapter techniques for creating containers, constructing topiary shapes, cutting and caring for flowers, forcing bulbs and branches, and making table-top gardens.

Equipping yourself

The list of tools and materials Ronaldo uses is relatively short. Still, you may not feel you need all of them, and the quantity of certain materials you keep on hand will be determined largely by the amount of space you have to store them. You may also wish to include additional equipment. There are, for example, many different kinds of devices for holding and positioning flowers in a container. Ronaldo does not use them, but you may find one or another of them helpful. In the discussion of each item on the list is a suggestion as to where you might be able to buy it locally. In addition, there is at the end of the chapter a list of sources where each can be ordered by mail.

A sharp knife is the one indispensable tool. Ronaldo, like most professionals, uses a florist's knife, a short-bladed, blunt-tipped knife that is sold with either a fixed blade or a folding one. The latter is usually a bit more expensive but can be tucked in pocket or purse for field-flower-gathering expeditions. If you cannot find a florist's knife—or an equivalent blade by another name—at a hardware or garden center, ask your local florist if he will order one for you.

Additional cutting tools—scissors, wire cutters, a small saw—will be needed from time to time, but they are standard household gear and while it is convenient to have a separate set for flower arranging, it is not essential.

Chicken wire is what Ronaldo uses most often to support and position flowers in a container, either alone or in combination with water-absorbent plastic foam. It is a hexagonal wire mesh, two feet wide, that is sold by the foot at most hardware stores. There is a green-coated version made specifically for flower arranging, but it is harder to find, more expensive, and rarely used by professionals. You need not keep a large supply on hand—three or four feet is enough for dozens of arrangements, especially since a piece can be reused several times. A professional trick: as soon as you bring it home, cut it in half lengthwise. The narrower width is easier to work with, and a foot-high coil easier to store than a two-foot one.

Water-absorbent plastic foam comes in bricks 3-by-4-by-9 inches, which you can buy individually or by the case of twenty-four, a saving if you use it frequently. Two well-known brand names are Oasis and Snowpak. Foam is also sold in 3-inch precut disks, but these are not really practical unless you have many containers three inches in diameter, and not necessarily even then, for the foam is soft and easy to cut. It must be thoroughly saturated before it is placed in the container. The easiest way to do this is to put a brick in a sink or pail full of water and leave it until it sinks to the bottom, which it will do when the water has penetrated to the center. Then let it drain for a few minutes until the excess water runs off. Once in the container it should be kept continually moist: if foam is allowed to dry out it does not reabsorb moisture readily. Foam is usually not reusable. It is not resilient and the holes made by stems are permanent, but it is particularly valuable for supporting flowers that have very slender or soft stems, for creating mock gardens, for designs where some stems must be placed above the rim of a container.

Raffia, which Ronaldo almost invariably uses to tie flowers to each other or to a support, is an individual preference, not a normal part of the florist's kit. It is a real discovery, easy to work with, soft enough not to cut or bruise flower stems, and very decorative. Most of the raffia available from craft suppliers is a synthetic imitation. It will do in a pinch, but the real

thing, definitely preferable, is made of palm fiber. It is often sold by horticultural suppliers for use in grafting.

Green-enameled florist's wire, which is nearly invisible and does not rust, is indispensable for making and hanging wreaths and garlands, binding moss or leaves onto topiary forms, and in fact for almost any fastening job that does not involve flower stems. It comes both in straight twelve- or eighteen-inch pieces and coiled on spools. Ronaldo finds the latter much more useful. Straight pieces are intended for straightening or shaping flower stems, a technique he almost never employs. He does use straight wire to create stems for nearly stemless flowers like gardenias and camellias, so that they can be pinned in the hair or to a dress, or tucked in a garland. If you only need an occasional spool it is better to buy one from your local florist, as most florist's supply companies will only sell it in very large quantities.

Floral clay, or preferably the similar but easier-to-use new adhesive that comes in paper-wrapped coils, is another useful product to keep on hand. Ronaldo uses it for sticking leaves or matting to containers and flowerpots. It is among the most widely available of florist's supplies and can often be found in variety stores.

Green stem-wrapping tape, paper or plastic, also quite easy to find, is used to keep stems from drying out when flowers must be kept out of water. It is employed primarily to prepare flowers for wearing or carrying in the hand. It comes in useful when you want to tuck flowers into wreaths or garlands and for some kinds of topiary or dried arrangements when water picks are too large or unavailable.

Water picks, which give each individual flower its own water supply, keep flowers better than stem-wrapping tape, in Ronaldo's opinion, and wherever possible he uses them. Water picks, which also go by the name of water vials, are small tapered plastic containers with caps of rubber or flexible plastic that form a watertight seal around the stems pushed through them. Most florists will sell you a few, or if you want a larger supply will order for you.

Flower picks, which sound similar, are something quite different. These are sharp-pointed, green-dyed wooden sticks with a length of fine wire attached at the blunt end. They are used to support soft flower stems in foam-based arrangements. For example, if the tulips you want to use in a moss basket seem to insist on bending over too much, you can attach the bottom two or three inches of stem to a flower pick before you insert it into the foam. They are also used a great deal in artificial flower arrangements. Flower picks come in several lengths and can sometimes be found packaged in variety stores.

Green moss has to be included in Ronaldo's list of basic equipment, for he uses it constantly. Live sheet moss is what you want to buy—the dyed dry kind is not nearly as attractive or as versatile. The moss will keep indefinitely in a plastic bag in the refrigerator, and four or five pounds do not take up much room. Moss that has simply been spread over the top of an arrangement or a pot of bulbs and kept moist can be reused several times. It is impractical to dismantle a topiary structure or a covered container for the sake of its moss, but since moss dries to a pleasant golden brown, any of these objects can themselves be reused. Not all florists carry live sheet moss, but it can be ordered by mail.

Charcoal helps keep the water in a container sweet and clear, and is especially useful for long-lasting arrangements of foliage. One lump of medium size or a spoonful of small ones is all it takes. Much of the charcoal sold for barbecues has been chemically treated and will not work, but because charcoal is also used to keep the soil sweet in plant pots it is almost always available

where potting supplies are sold.

A plant mister belongs on any list of flower-arranging equipment, although it is used to refresh and preserve an arrangement rather than in its construction. Anyone who keeps plants in the house should have one. The cheapest and most efficient ones are plastic bottles with trigger-operated sprayers and adjustable nozzles. They can be found in many supermarkets and most variety stores.

Woven grass matting is one of Ronaldo's favorite container coverings. It goes by a variety of names. We generally refer to it as tatami, but only when the matting is bound and padded do Japanese call it tatami; the plain matting is correctly called goza and comes in pieces 35 inches wide and 65 inches long. The Chinese version is called China matting and comes four feet wide and five, six, or seven feet long. All these distinctions are helpful to know when ordering it if you cannot find it at a local oriental shop. With a supply of matting at hand you can transform anything that holds water into an attractive flower container.

Natural bamboo canes about a half-inch in diameter and sawn into appropriate lengths are the raw material for miniature fences and container bases. Bamboo in the specific size you want may be difficult to find, but try stores that sell oriental goods. If you cannot locate it you can substitute wooden dowels from the lumberyard—Ronaldo often makes supports for smaller containers from quarter-inch ones—or bark-covered fruit-tree branches, which he also uses for the same purposes.

Plaster of Paris and Styrofoam are not on the basic list but should be mentioned because Ronaldo sometimes uses them to anchor topiary structures in their containers. They are so easy to obtain that you need not buy them until you need them. Variety stores carry Styrofoam in blocks, sheets, and various precut shapes; hardware and drugstores carry plaster of Paris.

Creating containers

The invented containers that give such a distinctive look to many of Ronaldo's flower designs are for the most part ordinary household objects—bowls, pails, baking tins—given new and decorative coverings. Here he demonstrates how to cover a container with grass matting, with leaves, and with moss, using as an example a straight-sided transparent plastic refrigerator jar; how to turn a moss-covered container into a basket with the addition of a branch handle, and then one way to fill it with flowers; and how to wrap a glass-globe vase with fabric.

To cover a container with grass matting or tatami:

1. Spread out the grass matting and, using the container as a guide, mark the width of the covering strip with a pencil. Measure the circumference of the container to find the length, adding about an inch extra.

2. Using a sharp scissors, cut the covering strip.

3. Press strips of florist's adhesive clay around the container, one about an inch from the top, the other about an inch from the bottom.

4. Wrap the strip of matting around the container, pressing it firmly to the adhesive.

5. Fold back the end of the strip to make a smooth edge, lap it over the other end, and anchor it with a dab of adhesive.

6. With the container on its side, wrap two or three long strands of raffia around it about an inch from the top, knot them tight, and then tie them in a bow.

7. Tie another double or triple strand of raffia half an inch or so from the bottom.

8. The finished container.

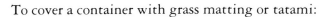

To cover a container with leaves:

1. Prepare the container by banding it top and bottom with florist's adhesive. Place the first leaf with its tip at the rim of the container and stem end at the bottom and press firmly to the adhesive. Large glossy magnolia leaves are used for the demonstration, but the technique is the same for galax or fern—or any leaf you choose. With smaller leaves, however, additional strips of adhesive will have to be applied to the container.

2. Continue adding leaves around the container, overlapping them and adjusting the tips to form an attractive pattern at the rim.

3. Pick up the container, and holding it carefully to avoid breaking the tips, trim off the stem ends evenly with scissors.

4. Twist several strands of raffia into a rope, knot the rope tightly around the container, tie the ends into a bow and fluff out the loops.

5. The finished container.

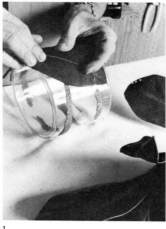
1

2

3

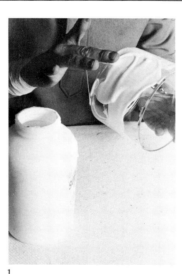
4

5

To cover a container with moss:

1. Smear the container evenly all over with a white all-purpose glue like Sobo. Let dry a minute or so until it is tacky. NOTE: Strips of florist's adhesive clay should be used to stick on the moss when you are covering a planted terra-cotta pot. Clay pots are porous and exude enough moisture to prevent glue from drying. Otherwise the technique is the same.

2. Take a large piece of live sheet moss and press it around the container. Rarely will you have a piece of moss large enough to wrap a container completely in a single operation.

3. Trim off the excess moss, holding the wrapping firmly in place.

4. Press on the trimmed-off moss to complete the covering.

5. Wrap the container round and round with green enameled wire, twist the wire ends together to fasten, and clip. With scissors, trim the moss evenly at the top and bottom of the container.

1

2

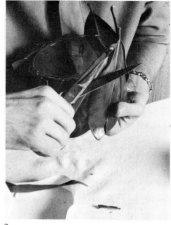
3

4

5

227

To turn the moss-covered container into a basket:

1. Take two twiggy branches of the same length and bind them to opposite sides of the container with wire. Any kind of branch can be used as long as it is not brittle and will bend without breaking.

2. Bend the branches across each other over the center of the container at whatever height seems right for the design you are planning.

3. Twine the branches into an arch, wrapping each tip around the opposite branch. Usually the twigs tangle and hold the arch together without any additional fastening, but if it seems unsteady or you want a more compact handle, a couple of strategically placed twists of wire or ties of raffia can be added.

1

2

3

With the moss basket finished, Ronaldo demonstrates one easy way to arrange flowers in it, using chicken wire as the foundation for the arrangement. Presoaked foam, trimmed to shape, would be substituted for the wire if the flowers to be arranged had very fine or very delicate stems.

1. Squeeze a piece of chicken wire into a rough ball. For a container of this size a piece approximately a foot square is about right.

2. Stuff the ball of chicken wire into the container.

3. Fill the container with water.

4. Place galax leaves around the rim of the container, letting each leaf overlap its neighbor.

5. Fill in the center of the container with galax leaves, adding just enough of them to conceal the chicken wire. They should not be packed too tight. You can always add one or two to the finished arrangement to hide an exposed patch of wire.

6. Start placing the flowers, beginning with the tallest. Ronaldo begins in the center with the tulip, which he knows will bend in the container. By the time he is ready to insert the last flower the tulip will show its inclination and can be balanced.

228

1

2

3

4

5

6

7 and 8. Add the rest of the flowers one by one, turning the container as you work to keep the composition balanced. The more you arrange flowers, the more easily you will be able to judge exactly what length to cut the stems before you place them in the container. An informal arrangement like this is good for practicing: it is easy to pull out stems and recut them to get the design you want.

9. With the placement of the last daisy, this arrangement of one pale-pink tulip, one red anemone, one pink nerine, two orangy-pink alstroemeria, and three white daisies is complete.

7

8

9

To slipcover a glass globe vase with fabric:

1. Spread a square of fabric, in this case a batik napkin, flat on work surface and place vase in the center. Cut two short lengths of wire from spool.

2. Pull two opposite edges of the napkin up to the rim of vase. The fabric should overlap the rim a little bit on both sides.

3. Holding these two edges in place with one hand, draw up the centers of the two remaining edges of fabric to the rim and hold. Pull out the corners in even folds.

4. With your free hand, gather the fabric on one side tightly and hold. The other hand can now release the fabric. With this hand pick up a length of wire, pass it under the holding fingers, draw tight around the gathered fabric, and fasten with a twist. This is more complicated to explain than to do, but you may have to try it a time or two before you get the knack of it.

5. Repeat the procedure on the other side, which is much easier because you have both hands free.

6. Adjust the folds, wrap strands of raffia over the wire bindings to conceal them, and tie in bows.

1

2

3

4

5

6

Constructing topiary forms

Many of Ronaldo's stylized arrangements take their inspiration from the topiaries achieved in the garden by a slow process of pruning and training trees and shrubs into geometric or animalistic shapes. His are more quickly achieved. Sometimes he simply gathers a mass of green stems in a container and clips it into shape with a scissors, but most of his spheres, arches, cones, animals and birds have structures of chicken wire and foam as underpinnings. More open forms may have only a framework of wire. He demonstrates both of the latter techniques with simple shapes. More complex ones, like animals and birds, are made on the same principle but may require wiring together several separately made forms.

To make a topiary ball:

1. Take a cube-shaped piece of foam—about half a brick—and wrap a piece of chicken wire twelve inches wide and about thirty inches long around it. Use dry foam. The shape can be soaked after it is finished.

2. Squeeze the chicken wire into a roughly symmetrical ball, turning it as you squeeze.

3. The foam cube in its chicken-wire cage. If you want the foam to hold moisture, soak it at this stage. Usually, however, Ronaldo places the stems of the flowers he will use to decorate the form in water picks and the foam is only there to give support to the water picks.

4. Cover the ball with sheet moss.

5. Take a spool of green florist's wire and wrap it round and round the moss until you have a smooth surface.

6. Poke flowers into the ball. You can do this before you set the ball on its stem, as shown, but it is usually easier to place the flowers decoratively after the following step. If the ball has been soaked and the flowers have stiff stems you can stick them straight in, but usually Ronaldo prefers to place flowers first in water picks, as he has the daisy in the illustration.

1

2

3

4

5

6

7. Holding the ball in both hands, push it down firmly onto its previously prepared stem, in this case a sturdy branch fixed in a square container with moss-covered plaster of Paris. Ronaldo does not always anchor stems this permanently. If the topiary were somewhat shorter and the container deeper—a flowerpot, for example—he might pack the container tightly with Styrofoam and wedge the stem into that.

7

To make a foam-and-wire cone:

This basic structure can serve a great many different arrangement purposes. Blocks of water-soaked foam are piled up in the container—here a lightweight plastic one—and taped together. Then a length of chicken wire is wrapped around the rim of the container, lashed in place with florist's wire, and squeezed into a tall cone. This particular pyramid of foam and chicken wire was fabricated to support the bouquet carried by a cherub in Chapter 5. Mounding foam and wire above the rim of a container is a technique used whenever you want to make an arrangement in which some of the stems are placed at a downward-slanting angle. The soft, wet foam keeps the stems moist, the dome of wire—which does not have to be this tall for most arrangements—supports them. This same shape, however, could as easily be the foundation for a cone-shaped topiary tree made of boxwood, moss, or holly.

1

2

3

4

5

6

To make a miniature heather-and-wire topiary:

1. Take three straight pieces of wire about twelve inches long. The wire should be soft enough to bend but stiff enough to hold its shape when bent. Most green-enameled florist's wire is too thin; suitable wire can be found at a hardware store.

2. With your fingers bend the wires into the desired curve, leaving a small straight piece at the top and a longer one at the bottom.

3. The wires bent to shape.

4. With florist's stem-wrapping tape, bind the three wires together at top and bottom.

5. Spread the wires apart to shape the frame.

6. Hold a spray of heather along one wire to gauge the length of stem you will need.

7. Cut six stems to the proper length and bunch together.

8. Bind the bunch of stems tightly to the stem of the frame with stem-wrapping tape.

9. Wind two stems of heather round and round each piece of wire and fasten with a twist of wire at the top. If the wires do not seem to be covered thickly enough, bind on as many more sprays of heather as you need to achieve the thickness you want.

10. Trim the tips into a topknot, and place the finished topiary in its container—here, a foam-filled, galax-wrapped candle glass.

7

8

9

10

Care and Conditioning of Flowers

It is nature in the end that determines the keeping quality of flowers. By working with nature, giving flowers the care they need and an atmosphere they like, you can bring out their best behavior, but some kinds simply last longer than others. Growing conditions—too much or too little moisture, too much or too little sun, overfeeding—can affect their longevity. Not all these factors are within your control even when you grow your own flowers; when you buy them, the quality of their previous care introduces still another variable. You can give your flowers the best treatment and still have disappointments occasionally—daffodils that shrivel, roses that wilt, lilies that shatter in a day. Such disappointments should not discourage you. The value of endurance in flowers or arrangements must be kept in perspective: the pleasure they give is really more important than how long that pleasure lasts.

In decorating with flowers you very often have to balance longevity against effectiveness. The life of the best-grown, best-conditioned, sturdiest flower will be shortened if it is placed right under a table lamp, yet that may be the very setting that shows it to best advantage. The problem may not be that dramatic. The normal conditions in most of our rooms, especially in winter—drafts and hot, dry air—are the enemies of flowers. Some react more quickly than others, but all suffer, and the reason is quite simple when you think about it. Plants, like human beings, exhale moisture through their pores, and transpiration in plants like perspiration in humans is accelerated by heat—and in plants by light as well. Drafts and dry air remove this moisture more rapidly than it can be replaced by normal intake. Flowers wilt, our skin dries out. Lowering the heat and raising the humidity in a room will do a great deal to make flowers last longer. Drafts cannot always be eliminated if you are to have any air

circulation, but you can usually avoid placing flowers in their direct path. Whatever the atmosphere of the room, you can give flowers some life-saving humidity by spraying them with a fine mist of water at least once a day. Flowers in hot spots—near lamps or in bright sunlight—can use it more frequently. Misting flowers—and it should be a very fine mist, since large drops of water will spot some petals—supplements but does not replace keeping up the water level in their containers. This should be checked at least once, preferably twice a day. The great majority of flowers absorb most of their water through the stems, and once a flower is cut its life and appearance depend almost completely on how well it is supplied with water. In addition to giving your flowers plenty of water after they are arranged, there is a good deal you can do before they are arranged to prepare them so that they can absorb it more easily.

Proper preparation of flowers begins with the cutting. And for cutting a sharp knife is much, much better than scissors. Scissors, however sharp, crush some of the cells in the stem through which the flower takes up water, thereby depriving the blossom of part or all of its supply. Flower stems should be cut at a sharp angle, not straight across. A long, slanting cut not only exposes more water-conducting cells to the water, it also ensures that they are exposed even when the stem is resting against the bottom of the container.

Sometimes in the garden scissors or pruning shears are much easier to use; for example, when you are cutting thorny stems or very thick woody ones. In such cases all you have to do is recut the stems with a knife before you place them in water.

When you cut is important if you are cutting flowers in the garden or in the wild. Cutting in the early morning or at the end of the day—late afternoon or early evening—will produce stronger flowers than cutting at midday when they have lost a great deal of moisture to the heat of the sun. They will also be stronger if you bring a pail of water to the garden with you and place them in it as soon as you cut them. Some may need additional preparation later, but even those suffer less from moisture loss if placed in water immediately. This is not always practical, particularly when you have to travel some distance, as you often do when cutting meadow and roadside flowers. In this case a supply of plastic bags and some damp cloths or paper toweling to wrap the stems will help sustain them until they can be put in water.

The stage of development at which you cut is really a matter of personal preference and the purpose you have in mind for your flowers. Most authorities recommend that for longest vase-life you cut when a bud is just about to open or has just opened, and let the blossom come to maturity in the vase. This can be important when you are fixing flowers for a party and want them to reach their peak of perfection at a specified time. Ronaldo, for example, buys flowers for a party two days ahead so that he can bring them to the exact stage he wants for his decorations. When you are picking flowers for everyday enjoyment, however, and have a constant source of supply in the garden, you can cut at any stage that suits you. True, flowers cut in tight bud may never fully open, but they may be just what you want for a design as they are. And you may want to enjoy the blossoms as long as possible in the garden before cutting them at full maturity for a day or two's enjoyment indoors. Fully developed flowers do need very careful handling, particularly the many-petaled ones. The loss of just one petal sometimes unzips the whole blossom. One more note about cutting in the garden: whenever there are leaves on the flower stem it is best for the plant to cut just above a leaf-node—the point where the leaf joins the stem—and to leave some foliage on the plant. In cutting roses, for example, it is considered

sound practice to leave at least two five-leaflet leaves on a stem. But for the sake of the cut flower it is best to cut just below the leaf node. This is a case where compromise—cutting between nodes—does nothing for either plant or flower. The answer is to cut for the plant and then recut the flower stem below a node before you condition it.

Conditioning is the next stage in good flower preparation. Its purpose is to help flowers absorb as much moisture as possible to replace the fluids they no longer receive from the plant. They may survive without it, but they rarely last as long or look as fresh, and proper conditioning can often revive flowers that seem hopelessly wilted—often but not always, which is why it is best to prevent wilting in the first place. Because some flowers have more difficulty than others in absorbing moisture, there is no one way to condition all flowers. In fact, the best way to treat each different kind is a subject of endless discussion and experiment among commercial growers, florists, horticulturalists, and experienced flower arrangers. They try everything—one prize-winning exhibitor at the Chelsea Flower Show in London reportedly conditions his carnations in lemonade—without reaching many definitive conclusions, although there are large areas of general agreement. Some of the more specialized techniques are worth investigating if you are interested in exhibiting in flower shows, but for day-to-day living and decorating with flowers they are not usually necessary. The suggestions for conditioning that follow, based on our experience, require no addition of chemicals to the water, but if you have found that adding sugar or vinegar or one of the commercial conditioning compounds works for you, by all means continue to use it. We have not found that they make much difference, but water varies widely in acidity and mineral content from place to place.

For a great many kinds of flowers conditioning is a relatively simple matter—the exceptions will be discussed separately. It involves cutting the flowers properly, removing all the foliage from the part of the stems that you think will be below the waterline in the finished arrangement, and placing them immediately in a container filled with water at least up to the leaf-line and preferably up nearly to the base of the flower—unless leaves are very soft they will survive submersion for a few hours—and leaving them for anywhere from four to twenty-four hours in a dark or at least shady, cool, draft-free place. One argument for cutting in the late afternoon is that you can condition your flowers overnight, sufficient time for most kinds, before arranging them. The first steps in the process can be taken as you cut in the garden if you take a container of water with you. It need not be filled to the brim; you can top it up after you bring it in. If you do not take water to the garden, then the stems should be recut before you immerse them. This is important. When flowers are left out of water for even a short time after cutting, the cells at the tip may dry out and become inefficient absorbers of water, or air bubbles may form over them and block the intake of moisture. For this reason some people, Japanese flower arrangers in particular, advocate recutting the stems under water. However, a Japanese friend tells us that this is in large part owing to a traditional belief that flowers belong to water, not air, and should therefore be cut in the element to which they belong. In our experience simply recutting them and placing them in water immediately works just as well.

What temperature should the water be? There is a great variety of opinion on this point, but it is our feeling—one shared by many commercial growers—that it should be as close as possible to the temperature of the air where the flowers are cut. Separation from the plant is a shock to flowers, and like most living things they react poorly to shocks. Conditioning should cushion, not add the further shock of a sudden change in temperature. Some flowers,

iris and forget-me-nots for example, will very quickly succumb to temperature changes. Bringing water to air temperature is very easy, you have only to let it stand in a container, outdoors or in, for a half hour. Some of the treatments advised for special categories of flowers may seem to be in the nature of shocks, but they are the best way of overcoming the problems caused by the structures of those particular plants. The most important exception to conditioning flowers in air-temperature water is when flowers are badly wilted. Then warm water, 100 to 110 degrees, which feels warm but not uncomfortable to the hand, seems to do a better job of reviving them.

You do not need special containers for conditioning flowers—anything deep enough for the length of the stems will do—but the containers you use should be scrupulously clean. Bacteria inevitably proliferate in water that contains plant stems, which exude fluids that provide bacteria with ample nourishment. Like air bubbles, bacteria will eventually block the flower's water intake, and if any are left in a container after previous use they have a head start on their destructive work. Ronaldo prefers glass containers for conditioning and keeping flowers; they are easier to keep clean than metal and many flowers react badly to metal containers. For household use plastic pails, cans, and hampers are equally good, easier to carry around, and can be found in sizes to fit even the tallest flowers.

If the plant material—flower or foliage—that you wish to condition is listed among the special categories that follow or is similar in structure to those in one of them, use the technique described for that kind of material. Almost all others respond to the procedure outlined above. If one does not, then recut the stems and treat it with warm water.

Plants with woody stems—trees, shrubs, woody vines—need more cells exposed to water than a slanting cut can provide. Using a sharp knife, cut several slits in the stems, up to about two or three inches from the ends, before placing in air-temperature water for conditioning. Hammering instead of splitting is often recommended, but it has only one advantage—speed—and many disadvantages. Smashed stems are more difficult to position, look unattractive in a container, and inevitably some of the stem is crushed or torn free and decays in water. When woody branches have both leaves and flowers, they will look and last better if most or all of the leaves are removed. Removing all leaves is usually recommended for lilacs, but in our experience they last longer if the one leaf-cluster nearest the flower panicle is left on. It seems to help draw water up to the flowers. Condition leafy branches separately if you want foliage for your design. Some commonly used material that takes this treatment:

> *Trees:* beech, dogwood, eucalyptus, evergreens, fruit trees, maple, oak.
> *Shrubs:* azalea, forsythia, honeysuckle, hydrangea, lilac, mock orange, mountain laurel, pussy willow, pyracantha, rose of Sharon, spirea, weigela.
> *Vines:* clematis, silverlace, wisteria. Special cases: Bougainvillea—submerge completely in cool water until crisp. Mimosa—split stems, cover blooms with a plastic bag, place stems in a container of boiling water and leave until ready to arrange.

Plants with fibrous stems which seem woody but are not bark-covered should also have stems split before conditioning in air-temperature water.

> *Examples:* artemisia, fuchsia, lantana, peony, phlox, santolina and most herbs, sunflower. Special cases: carnations—leave all foliage on stem. Cutting under water in conditioning container is sometimes beneficial. Chrysanthemums, including Shasta daisies, Michaelmas daisies, marguerites. Scrape stems, cut ends on slant, remove all leaves that will be below waterline, but leave some on

stem if possible. Condition in air-temperature water.
> Roses—remove thorns, cut on slant, condition in air-temperature water. Use warm-water treatment if they droop.

Plants that exude a sticky liquid from their stems—white, yellow, or colorless—can be treated in one of two ways. Either slit the stem for about an inch and hold it in the flame of a match, a cigarette lighter, or a gas burner while you count to fifteen slowly, or place two inches of stem-end in a pot of boiling water and hold it there for the same count. If you use the latter method you will have to wrap the flowers in paper to protect them from the steam and the heat of the burner. A good method is to cut a slit in several thicknesses of newspaper, poke the stems through and gather the newspaper loosely up around the flowers. If you have only a few flowers to prepare the flame method is easier, but with a quantity the boiling method, where you can do several at once, saves time. After the stem-ends have been seared or boiled, place flowers in air-temperature water and condition for six or eight hours. When you are working with flowers of this kind, try to estimate the length of stem you will need for your arrangement. If the stems have to be cut shorter, they will again have to be seared or boiled. The reason for this curious procedure is that heat solidifies the sticky liquid quickly and keeps it in the cells that produce it. If it is allowed to flow out and cover the ends of the stem it will block the water-conducting cells as it solidifies. Some of the flowers that need this treatment are:

> Butterfly weed, Canterbury bells, cardinal flower, dandelion, all the euphorbias including poinsettia, and hollyhock, milkweed, oleander, oriental poppy, platycodon, plumeria, stephanotis.

Plants with fleshy, succulent stems, which are sometimes hollow, should be conditioned in cold water. Most but not all of these are flowers produced by bulbs or corms. If the stem has a solid white section at the bottom, remove this or cut a slit through it. Otherwise, cut on a slant.

Examples: allium, amaryllis, anemone, balsam, bleeding heart, clivia, grape hyacinth, hyacinth, lily of the valley, nasturtium, nerine, portulaca, scilla.
Special cases: cyclamen—pull flower stems from plant instead of cutting. Split stems, condition in cold water.
Daffodils and jonquils—dip first in warm water, then condition in cold water. They last better when arranged in shallow water.
Gladiolus—leave out of water a half-hour before conditioning. Surprisingly, this flower benefits from slight wilting. Placing stems slantwise in the conditioning container will make them curve.
Irises do not like temperature changes. Condition in air-temperature water, preferably as close as possible to that of the room in which they will be finally placed.
Tulips and calla lilies—wrap in a collar of paper during conditioning to keep stems straight. They will still bend somewhat when arranged.

Some plant materials should be conditioned by *complete submersion in water.* For these the water should be cold and the conditioning period much briefer—two to four hours for leaves, usually not more than a few minutes for flowers.

Leaves: bamboo, caladium, ferns, galax, grape ivy, ivy, and most soft fleshy leaves like skunk cabbage. Leafy vegetables. The leaves of root vegetables like beets, carrots, turnips.

Flowers: tuberous begonias, camellias, gardenias, magnolias all absorb part of their moisture through their petals. Holding the stem, dip the blossom gently into cold water for a few minutes, lift out and hold at an angle

or shake very gently to let excess water run off. Keep covered on a bed of moist cotton in a cool place until ready to arrange. Mist frequently. If you are working with whole branches of camellia, gardenia, or magnolia they should be conditioned like the woody stems they are. Rhododendron, yucca, and canna lilies—submerge stem and flowers until crisp, usually between one-half and two hours, then place in cold water. Violets—tie in bunches, hold under water until crisp, 15 minutes to an hour—then place stems in cold water. Mist violets very frequently.

NOTE: Some flowers which might appear to take similar treatment will be badly damaged if their petals are placed in water or sprayed. The most common of these are orchids, lilies, sweet peas, and baby's breath.

These conditioning techniques are intended primarily for flowers that you cut yourself, but they are also useful for the flowers you buy. The flowers in a flower shop should have been prepared and conditioned by the grower and reconditioned by the florist when he received them. Unfortunately, this is not always the case. It takes time to prepare and condition flowers properly. Some florists and most street vendors just stick them in water without even recutting stems. If you buy or are given flowers that have not been prepared—roses with thorns on the stems, branches that have not been split—it pays to prepare and recondition them. They need not stand in deep water more than a couple of hours before arranging. In fact, it is a good idea to recut and recondition all florist's flowers unless they are already arranged in a container, because it is hard to tell how long they have been out of water before reaching you. Place flowers in warm water— 100 to 110 degrees—for reconditioning unless they are the kind that must be seared or boiled, or have succulent stems, or should be submerged in water. For these three categories reconditioning is the same as conditioning.

Creating gourd containers

Finding ready-made gourd containers like those Ronaldo uses—his come from Brazil—is not easy. Most of those that turn up for sale in this country have been carved or painted, and it is the naturalness and simplicity of the plain ones that make them such appealing flower containers. If you can find gourds of the right kind, however, making them into containers is a fairly simple process. The hard-shell gourds used to make containers are varieties of *Lagenaria leucantha* and are usually green or pale greenish white, turning golden brown when dried or touched with frost. Sometimes they appear in late autumn at farmers' markets or roadside stands, but mostly you find there only the brightly colored ornamental varieties of *Cucurbita pepo,* which are soft-shelled and unsuited to container-making.

If you have a garden the easiest way to get your gourds may be to grow them. Catalogues list them as easy to grow and give planting instructions but usually fail to point out that they need about 130 days of warm, frost-free weather to grow and mature; once matured, lagenarias are not harmed by frost. For gardeners in the northern part of the country this means that they are best started indoors in the spring and not set out until all danger of frost is past.

Gourds must be dried before they are hollowed out. Leave a couple of inches of stem on the gourds when you cut them from the vine, wash them with soap and water, and hang them to dry by their stems in a warm, dry, well-ventilated place. They may take a couple of months to dry completely, depending on size. Check periodically and discard any with rotten spots, but if a little surface mold develops it can be removed with a stiff brush and soap and water.

When the gourds are thoroughly dried, container-making can begin. Decide where you want the opening to be and outline it in pencil on the gourd. With a sharp knife gradually cut away the gourd within the outline. Scoop and scrape out the interior, being careful not to pierce the shell. Sand the cut edge smooth and you have your flower container. If you want a glossy surface you can shellac or wax it, but this is not necessary. If you want to attach a base to it, as Ronaldo sometimes does, drill holes near the rim to receive cords or raffia ties.

Forcing flowering branches

Cut branches of spring-flowering shrubs and fruit trees can be brought into blossom indoors from two months to a month before their normal blooming date outdoors. To do this they must be cut from four to six weeks before you want them in bloom. Since each variety has a different blooming date—to compound the problem these blooming dates vary in different regions of the country and in different years—observation of the plant is the only way to tell when the buds have begun to swell a little on the branches and are ready for forcing. Start watching the earliest ones, like pussy willow and forsythia, in January and continue on through early spring for later varieties. With experience you will learn to recognize what degree of development will produce the best results. If buds shrivel and drop off indoors you have cut a little too soon, if the plant flowers outdoors before your cut branches, you have waited too long.

Cutting branches with care for the shape of the shrub or tree doubles the benefit: you not only speed up spring but take care of some necessary pruning.

Preparation of branches for forcing is like preparation for conditioning, but with the following differences: scrape about three inches of outer bark from stem ends as well as slitting them. Submerge the branches completely in room-temperature water—65 to 70 degrees—for twenty-four hours. Then place in a fairly deep container filled with cool water, with a piece or two of charcoal added to keep the water sweet. Place container in a semishady, draft-free location. Strong sun, heat, or drafts will dry out the buds before they can develop. Mist the branches at least once a day. Every week change the water and cut an inch or so from the stem end. When buds show color and are nearly open, moving the container to a sunny spot will give the flowers stronger color, but they will need additional misting.

If, after two to four weeks depending on the variety, the flowers seem to be lagging, you can hurry them along by refilling the container once a day with 100-degree water and misting them with warm water.

Forcing spring bulbs

Even if you live in a tiny apartment with an uncontrollable heating system you can force bulbs for winter bloom. A few of the most popular and beautiful kinds are quite undemanding. If you have a house and a garden the possibilities expand, and, with the addition of a cold frame and a greenhouse you can grow any bulb the catalogues suggest for forcing and even try some they have not thought of. These notes are confined to the easier kinds. They are the best to start with. Then, as you gain experience, you can adventure with the fussier ones.

Accurate watering is the real trick to forcing bulbs. Once they are planted in a container they must never be allowed to dry out, but too much water in the soil around a bulb or standing over its base will cause it to rot. Too much water is more often the cause of failures than too little, particularly in the early stages of forcing. After bulbs have developed a strong root system they can absorb and even need more moisture and will tolerate an occasional overwatering.

When bulbs are planted in pebbles, bulb fiber, or in special water glasses, the base of the bulb should be between a half and a quarter inch above the water level. But in these cases you can see the water level and tip any excess out of the container. When bulbs are planted in soil in terra-cotta or plastic pots it is much harder to tell. The surface may seem dry when it is in fact moist enough around the bulbs. One way to check is to poke in your finger an inch or so. Misting pots generously gives better control than pouring on water, but however you water bulbs be sure to pour off any excess that drains into the saucer. How frequently bulbs must be watered depends so much on the heat and humidity of the location that it is best to work out your own schedule. Testing every day or every other day for a week or so will tell you.

Proper planting helps make sure that bulbs receive the right amount of water. The drainage hole in the pot should be covered with a pot shard, convex side up, or with a layer of coarse pebbles for drainage. The soil line should be an inch below the rim of the pot. The soil should be a light one that drains easily. Most commercial potting soils will do but are improved by the addition of some sand. Soil and pot should be thoroughly moistened before planting. A handful of properly moist soil will form a ball when you squeeze it in your hand, but will instantly disintegrate when dropped back on the pile. To insure good drainage, growers who force bulbs for the florist market often put two or three inches of soil in the bottom of the pot, set the bulbs on top of it and then use pure sand to surround and cover the bulbs.

If your bulb has a flat side, set that side facing the outside of the pot. Leaves sprout from the flat sides.

Plant bulbs as soon as you receive them in the mail or buy them at a nursery. They do not keep well in normal household conditions. Some nurseries suggest that they can be kept in open plastic bags in the refrigerator and can be planted in succession, but placing several small orders to be sent in succession seems to work better. And in any case, even if you plant all the bulbs at once, they usually will not all blossom at once.

These techniques apply to all bulbs planted for forcing unless exceptions are noted in the discussion of specific varieties.

The easiest bulbs to force are those that do not require a cool prerooting period and are tolerant even of overheated rooms. They are, in ascending order of difficulty:

Amaryllis. Potted in early November, amaryllis will flower for Christmas if you buy specially precooled bulbs. Otherwise count on about eight weeks from planting. It likes rich soil, about one-third well-rotted cow manure. The pot size should allow an inch of soil around the circumference of the bulb. Place bulb so that half to two-thirds of it is above the soil surface. Put in warm, light but not sunny location and water moderately until a tip of green shows. Then begin watering more frequently and move to a place with more light. It does not need full sun, but when you have only north light it seems to do better with a boost from a plant light. Blossoms last a bit longer if the plant is moved to a cooler location when buds start to open, which is not always possible. Cut off flower stems as soon as blossoms fade. Amaryllis will blossom year after year if you keep watering them all summer, in the windowsill or planted in their pots in a partly shaded area in the garden. In mid September, turn pots on their sides—dig up if in the garden—in a shaded place outdoors or a well-ventilated closet indoors to let dry. In late October, cut off any remaining foliage, water the

pots, give a second watering with a solution of liquid fertilizer, and bring them into the room. They will again grow and bloom.

Narcissus. Paperwhite, Grand Soleil d'Or, Chinese sacred lily, February, or Cragford. These will flower about six weeks from planting. Plant in a container—it need not be more than two-and-a-half inches deep—filled with pebbles or bulb fiber. Set bulbs on at least one-and-a-half inches of pebbles, and place a little charcoal in the container to keep the water sweet. If you use bulb fiber—a mixture of coarse peat, charcoal, and oyster shell—keep the top third of the bulb uncovered. Or you can plant bulbs in soil in terra-cotta pots. Use the shallow ones called bulb pans, again keeping the top third of the bulb exposed. Keep in a warm dark place—under a bed, in a closet—until a good root mass has formed and the leaves are about six inches high. Check the water every two or three days. Bring the plants gradually into the light. After buds are well developed they can take full sunlight but they do not need it. Bulbs cannot be reused.

Hyacinth. French-Roman or Dutch. French-Roman hyacinths have delicate graceful flower spikes in white, blue, or pink. They have the same requirements and are forced in exactly the same way as narcissus, but they take a week or so longer to blossom. They can also be grown in special hyacinth glasses designed to hold the bulb above water. Bulbs are not reusable. Dutch hyacinth, with their familiar thickly flowered spikes, can be planted in hyacinth glasses, or, with the tip of the bulb uncovered, in bulb fiber or soil—the flower spikes are too heavy to work well in pebbles. You can sometimes buy specially prepared ones that will flower by Christmas if planted in late September or early October. Untreated ones take longer to blossom. Buy varieties suggested for forcing. Dutch hyacinths should be given a cool dark place to form their roots before being brought into warmth and light—a basement or garage, perhaps. In an apartment a really cool spot is harder to find, but hyacinths seem fairly tolerant of less than ideal conditions, especially if they are regularly misted. Some authorities feel that Dutch hyacinth should have a truly cold prerooting period (see below). It is not strictly necessary but it may produce taller, more spectacular blossoms. Bulbs cannot be forced again but can be planted in the garden.

Lily of the valley is not, strictly speaking, a bulb, but specially prepared pips are available that will blossom about twenty-one days from planting. Plant in bulb fiber or sphagnum moss with the tips of the sprouts just below the rim of the container—packed tightly in one that is six or seven inches deep or loosely with roots spread out in a shallower bowl or pot. Leave in a dark place about 60 degrees and water daily until the sprouts are about four inches tall. Bring gradually into the light and finally into full sun or in range of a plant light to flower. Mist frequently.

Almost all the other bulbs that can be forced in winter need a precooling period. This is most easily done if you have a garden. Plant bulbs in September or October in terra-cotta bulb pans or wood or plastic flats, large bulbs with the tips breaking the surface of the soil or sand, small ones lightly covered. Water thoroughly. Place outdoors in a pit, cold frame, or a packing box in a sheltered place and cover with leaves, straw, or sawdust. Temperatures should stay around 40 to 45 degrees, but if temperatures go below freezing for short periods they will not be harmed. In from four to eight weeks, depending on the kind, bulbs should be well rooted. Check by inverting a pot, tapping to free the earth ball in your open hand, removing the pot, and looking at the root mass. When soil is full of roots or shoots have risen an inch above the rim of the container, bring indoors and gradually into daylight. When buds develop, give them as much sun as possible. Apartment dwellers can achieve the same results by putting one or two pots in the vegetable compartment of the refrigerator. Open the compartment for a moment or two once a week to let

in a little fresh air and prevent mold from forming, which is the only problem in refrigerator bulb-cooling.

The following bulbs can all be forced easily by this method, but they prefer a cooler indoor temperature—about 65 degrees—than is maintained in many houses.

Daffodils, narcissus, and jonquils are among the easiest. Specially prepared bulbs of certain varieties planted in September or October can be forced for Christmas. For mid-winter flowering, bulbs do not need special preparation and flower in four to six weeks, depending on room temperature. Be sure to choose varieties recommended for forcing.

Also easy are small bulbs like allium neapolitanum, crocuses, snowdrops, grape hyacinths, all the miniature species daffodils, puschkinia or striped squill, scilla sibirica or blue squill, and star of Bethlehem.

Lilies. With modern refrigeration techniques many different lilies, including some of the colorful Mid-Century Hybrids, can be precooled for forcing. Growers who offer these prepared bulbs generally include instructions with the order— request them to make sure—since care differs with the variety.

Tulips are more demanding in matters of temperature. Choose specially prepared ones or varieties suggested for forcing. The lady tulip, *T. clusiana,* a tiny species tulip, can also be forced successfully although for some reason it is not usually suggested in catalogues.

Iris are tricky but a triumph when you succeed. Only the bulbous kinds—Dutch or species iris—can be forced. They need excellent drainage, plenty of light and water, and should not be moved once they are brought indoors for forcing —the plants, like the cut flowers, suffer from sudden temperature changes. Dutch iris really need a greenhouse, but the tiny purple iris reticulata and yellow iris danfordiae can be forced in a house or apartment if the conditions are to their liking.

Creating tabletop gardens

Miniature gardens planted in containers are not only enjoyable and easy to make, they are also one of the most attractive ways to decorate with forced bulbs and small flowering or foliage plants. The container can be almost anything you like as long as it is deep enough for both the bulb or plant and a good layer of gravel for drainage. One caution: silver or brass containers should have liners—chemicals in the soil may damage the finish.

The first step is to fill your container with about an inch of coarse gravel and sand. Tuck in a couple of medium-sized lumps of charcoal or a spoonful of smaller ones to keep soil and water sweet. Next, thoroughly moisten a nice light potting soil—one-half commercial potting soil, one-quarter peat, and one-quarter sand is a good formula. The next steps vary a bit depending on the kind of plant material and the composition you have in mind.

If you are planting bulbs, turn over the container they were grown in and tap out the root ball. Set on your work surface and gently separate the bulbs. If the roots do not untangle easily, cut rather than pull them apart. For a mass planting,

put in a thin layer of soil, set in the bulbs, fill in any gaps with soil, firm up, and give a good misting of water. This is also the technique when you have lifted a clump of plants like violets or marigolds from the garden.

If you are planning a more complex landscape involving several different plants—three crocuses and two tiny ferns in a moss lawn, for example—it is easier to compose the design using small empty pots or tumblers to determine the placement of the major elements. Once you have an arrangement that pleases you, leave the pots or tumblers in place and fill the container with soil. Remove the pots or tumblers and set in the bulbs or plants. Firm up the soil and mist. Press pieces of moss in place to cover the bare spots. Moss should be thoroughly moistened but not dripping. A garden like this, properly planted and watered, can go on for months, with bulbs or flowers removed and replaced as they fade. The crocuses in the example might be followed by pansies, little begonias, and marigolds or verbenas for a summer-long succession of bloom.

SOURCES FOR EQUIPMENT

Brookstone Company, 5 Vose Farm Road, Peterborough, New Hampshire 03458. Floral adhesive clay in rolls, stem-wrapping tape, water vials (picks), flower picks, dyed dry green moss, straight florist's wire. Write for "Hard-to-Find Gifts Catalogue."

Lun On Company, 771 Sacramento Street, San Francisco, California 94108. China matting, bamboo in a variety of sizes. Write for prices.

Mellinger's, Inc., 2310 West South Range,

North Lima, Ohio 44452. Florist's knives, raffia, live sheet moss, floral adhesive clay in rolls and in blocks, stem-wrapping tape, coiled florist's wire, straight florist's wire, green-enameled chicken wire, flower picks, Oasis, charcoal. Write for catalogue.

John Scheepers, Inc., 63 Wall Street, New York, N.Y. 10005. Live sheet moss, charcoal. Listed in catalogue "Beauty from Bulbs, Forcing Edition," or write for prices.

INDEX

Page numbers in *italics* indicate illustrations.